digital
illustration

WORK
HARD
&
BE NICE
TO PEOPLE

digital
illustration

a master class
in creative
image-making

Lawrence Zeegen

RotoVision

A RotoVision Book

Published and distributed by
RotoVision SA
Route Suisse 9
CH-1295 Mies
Switzerland

RotoVision SA
Editorial Office and Sales Office
Sheridan House
112/116A Western Road
Hove BN3 1DD, UK

Tel: +44 (0)1273 72 72 68
Fax: +44 (0)1273 72 72 69
Web: www.rotovision.com

10 9 8 7 6 5 4 3 2

ISBN: 2-88046-797-7

Art Director Luke Herriott
Design Russell Hrachovec and Ondrej Slezek at compoundEye
Picture research Ondrej Slezek

Reprographics in Singapore by Provision Pte.

Contents

Introduction

Today's innovators in graphic image-making have grown up with the digital, with a computer in every classroom. For some, it's worth recognizing that even before school, digital kit in the bedroom or the playroom has been the real starting point of their creativity.

Today's image-makers have not had to adapt to the changes that digital technology brought, but have developed their skills intuitively, utilizing the huge advances that have been made. Digital technologies are much more connected with everyday lives than ever before, and, for many, that connection starts from an earlier age. Young creatives no longer consider the computer "new." Having grown up with PlayStation, Nokia mobile phones, the Canon IXUS, and, more recently, the iPod, they understand the ins, the outs, the ups, and the downs of digital media. It is no coincidence that nowadays, a basic start-up computer package includes a scanner, printer, and digital camera alongside the computer itself. Increasingly, packages also include a wi-fi box and card, allowing instant Web access from anywhere in the home as well as bundled digital-manipulation software and royalty-free photographic images, clip-art and fonts; the "perfect" recipe ingredients. Encouraged to manipulate and create "visuals" from the outset, today's image-makers regard the computer, with its adjuncts, as "just another tool."

Access any Availability

Greater access to constantly improving hardware at ever-decreasing prices has helped drive the purchasing demand from the public. Over the past 15 years, "stack them high and sell them cheap" computer warehouses have appeared on the outskirts of every town and city across the computerized world. Drive in, speak to a "qualified expert," road-test some kit, make an educated choice, and scoot away with hardware and software more

1. Stephen Bliss, personal project, Bibahead T-shirt
2. ilovedust, personal project, White Yeti
3. Susannah Edwards, personal project, binary self-portrait poster
4. John Hersey, Greenpeace, Green Tax Incentives
5. Jason Ford, Brunswick PR, N is for New York

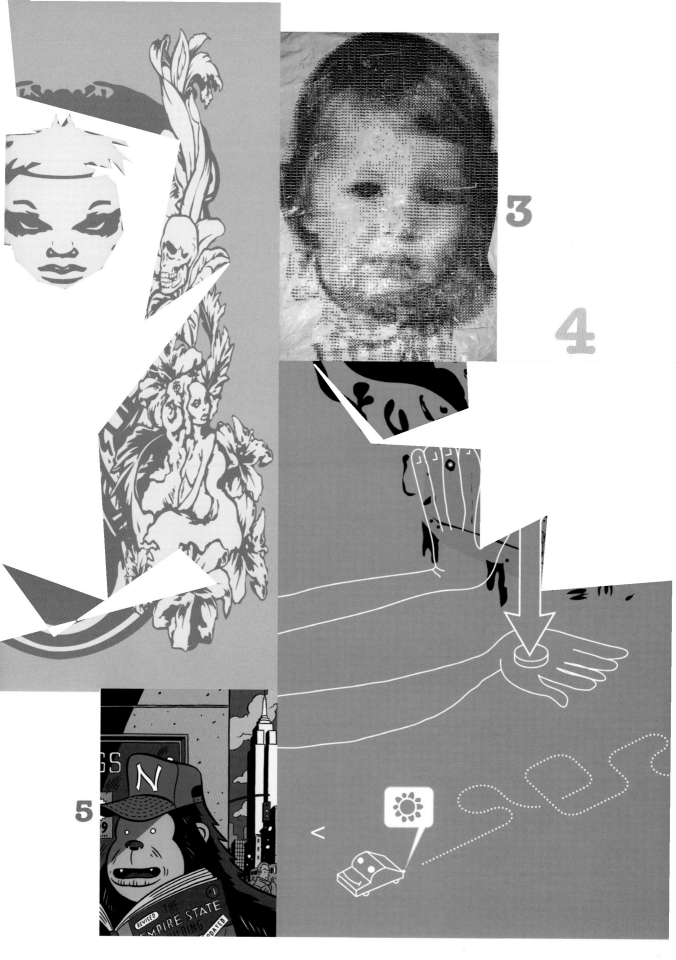

powerful than even governments had access to 20 years ago, at a price unthinkable just a decade ago. With the computer retail industry becoming increasingly cutthroat, buying a computer has never been cheaper or easier.

For those already within the digital loop—and that number rises daily—it is the issue of constant upgrading that requires attention, or so the manufacturers would like us to believe. No time to get to the warehouse? There is always the option of buying the necessary kit online, opting for "hassle-free, no-nonsense, next-day delivery" and "easy" deposit and payment terms to get your hands on the most up-to-date kit. Simplicity is the key.

6. Clarissa Tossin, *Grooves* magazine, Flower
7. ilovedust, Dave White, Artist's Shoes
8. Ray Smith, *GQ* magazine, Enlightenment
9. Simon Pemberton, *New Scientist* magazine, Gaming
10. Ian Wright, *GQ* magazine, Mike Tyson
11. John Hersey, *Fortune* magazine, Bad or Good Economy?
12. Joel Lardner, Fenchurch, spring/summer collection 2005

8

The Rise of Hardware and Software

And as the quality of available hardware continues to improve, so does the software industry's output. Creative imaging and manipulation software has become far more powerful and easier to use, with manufacturers recognizing a new market growing quietly alongside the traditional market of creative professionals. Modified versions of professional applications have been created for and marketed toward the creative home user. Neither a true professional image-maker, nor a complete novice, the home user is a motivated, skilled, and keen amateur. With greater computing experience than ever before, the home user has a wider range of basic skills from which to draw; with access to the latest hardware and software, the home user is able to approach the creation of digital image-making in an increasingly professional manner.

The explosion in the use and accessibility of both the Web and digital photography has also helped to fuel the rise in digital image-making. With the tools for manipulating digital photographs now readily available, many illustrators and designers have sought to increase their range of skills and move into areas closer to commercial digital illustration. For the home user looking to find an audience for their work, publishing on the Web has been the logical progression: it avoids print, production, and postage costs, which, in other media, can be frighteningly high; most e-mail hosts now offer cheap domain names and limited Web space; and Web-design software is now far easier to use than the raw hypertext mark-up language (HTML) required at the dawn of the Internet. Access to the Web increases daily as more and more users join the superhighway for the first time, and the speed of connections hits new highs as users ditch dial-up for broadband services.

In the analog world, magazine publishers have leapt to the challenge of creating monthly publications for digital image-makers and would-be Web designers, providing easy-to-read, step-by-step know-how in an instant. These give instructions for using software, and offer tips and tricks, with creative and technical advice alongside examples from industry professionals. Their readership figures easily surpass those of the pure and traditional design journals and magazines.

9

10   **11**

12

The Education of the Image-Maker

Art and design education has also contributed to the image-making boom. The number of graduates from creative design and media-related courses has risen dramatically in recent years. This is due both to the rapid growth in the number of courses offered and to the increase in student numbers, in response to demand. International competition for students is another contributing factor; many institutions have increased their annual spend on the digital, resulting in more fully equipped computer labs and better-informed teaching staff. In terms of choice, there has never been a better time to study communication design.

13

14

15

18

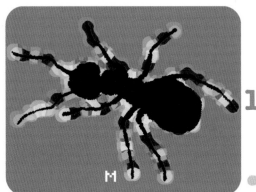

16

17

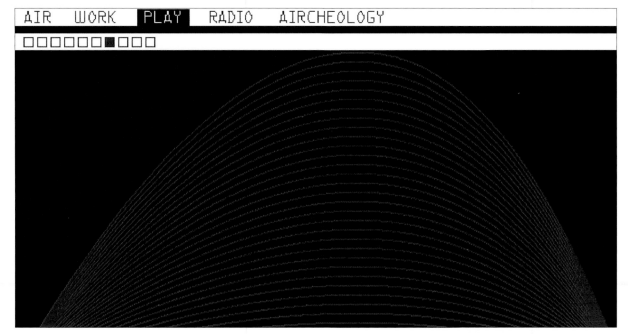

19

20

21

19. David Foldvari, *Grafik* magazine, Environments issue
20. Mick Marston, personal project, The Futile Vignettte company exhibition, New York
21. Richard May, *Computer Arts* magazine, cover image

Twenty-First Century Flux

At the start of the twenty-first century, professional image-making is in a state of flux. Cutting-edge graphic design, with its constant reinvention, demands new and innovative ways of visualizing concepts and bringing ideas, moods, and movements to life. The discipline had been struggling to find the next "big thing," a fresh look, ever since the excitement of digital typography, delivered in the mid-nineties, had begun to diminish, and the fashion for hyperrealist photography became overblown and overused toward the end of the decade.

Changes and developments in contemporary music and fashion often occur at street level, with cultural shifts led by small but influential groups of movers and shakers. The same is true for art and design. Away from the prying eyes of the media, new approaches and new visions start to emerge. The "style" press, often the purveyors of all things new, bright, and shiny, began to recognize and reflect new means of creating "cool" images. Previously creatively constrained by the sole use of photography, brave steps have been taken to break with tradition and to showcase work from the undercurrent of emerging image-makers.

Breaking Boundaries

Neither graphic designer, photographer, nor illustrator, these "graphic image-makers" have started to cross boundaries, creating their own visual languages, their own innovative brand of picture-making, to capture the essence of the stories they are commissioned to cover, and the products and artists they promote. They are providing the visual zeitgeist.

The secret of the most successful work lies in its artistic combination of the digital and the traditional in an unobtrusive and subtle manner. Using digital photographic techniques alongside or in combination with drawing and painting skills, and merging these with aspects of practice developed from printmaking, letterpress printing, stenciled street art and the like, this cutting-edge approach demands attention. A visual equivalent to the scratching, sampling, and remixing of contemporary music, this new esthetic draws upon many creative inspirations and techniques. Often working alone or in small studio set-ups, sometimes even as part of independent design studios, these mavericks have started to change the face of contemporary illustration and graphic design.

Section One:
Working Process

Underground Influences

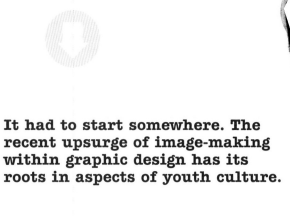

It had to start somewhere. The recent upsurge of image-making within graphic design has its roots in aspects of youth culture.

An undercurrent of fresh, raw talent has always been responsible for forcing disciplines forward. Music, for example, was altered with the Sex Pistols and punk in the seventies and Public Enemy and hip-hop in the eighties; the landscape changed forever, as new music shed its past and reinvented itself by and for a new generation. Movies did the same in breaking the mold; *Easy Rider* in the sixties and *Mean Streets* in the seventies radically affected and influenced a new generation of filmmakers. In the arts, Andy Warhol in the sixties and Damien Hirst in the noughties have had a similar effect on popular culture and on their contemporaries.

Rejuvenation and Reinvention
For the graphic image-maker too, a rejuvenation and reinvention of the medium echoes the changes across aspects of popular culture. As new methods, approaches, fashions, and ideas merged with new technologies and new creative and commercial outlets, so new methods of working have begun to emerge. Finding or creating a platform for new work has always been tricky: the commercial world rarely wants to take risks, preferring to use a visual language that is tried and tested. Therefore, when an outlet that works as a test bed for visual innovation—maintaining and driving change—is created, it is vital to recognize its strengths.

Style Wars
It may seem long ago now, and the event has lost some of its significance, but the birth of the "style" magazine in the UK—with the publication of *The Face* in May 1980— was an important and defining moment in the recording, reporting, and reflection of a popular culture regarded as "of interest" by the nation's youth. Here was a template that would later be borrowed, copied, or pillaged, depending on your stance, around the world. Within just

2

3

4

wow

5

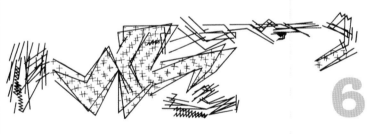

6

1. Billie Jean, *Native Weapon* magazine, Le Freak C'est Chic
2. Insect, Right Guard Xtreme Sport packaging
3. Andy Potts, Woodsuch Web site, Bubby 3-D
4. Insect, The Wooster Collective, Sin Clown
5. Walnut, *The Face* magazine, DeFace badges
6. Ian Wright, *The Face* magazine, Issue 01 Man

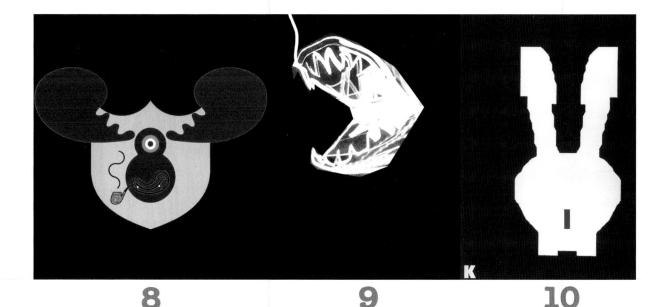

8   9   10

a few short years it was influencing not only others in magazine publishing, but also people across related fields including advertising, fashion, journalism, and design.

Design, and graphic design in particular, was high on the agenda in the era that dubbed itself The Designer Decade. It could be argued that it all began with that first issue of *The Face*, proclaiming itself "Numero Uno, licensed to thrill." Although the design was a little raw in places, it was clear that as well as reflecting popular youth culture, it would also play a part in defining it. Ahead of the British pack that was soon to include *i-D*, still going strong, and *Blitz* (a pale imitation of *The Face* that died a couple of years after its launch) the look and feel of *The Face* would go on to influence design in the US, notably in music magazines such as *Raygun*, and in the TV graphics for MTV.

7. Matthew Green, *Sleaze Nation* magazine, Ican'tbelieveitsnotbetter
8. Mick Marston, personal project, The Futile Vignette company exhibition, New York
9. Richard May, personal project, Carcharhinus leucas
10. Ian Wright, Tony Kaye, Bun Bun

The first issue of *The Face* featured just one image not created by the camera—a drawing by Ian Wright graced its contents page. The stark image of a zoot-suited man running, dancing, or perhaps chasing his hat, printed in simple black line, looked anything other than hand-drawn. Wright had produced an image which suggested that a computer had played some part in its creation. Jagged, edgy, almost digital in feel, though with a nod toward the work of Russian abstract artist Wassily Kandinsky, Wright's image looked both modern and youth-driven, with a hint of the digital, years before the technology would allow such work.

1984 and the Mac
The technology that would permit Wright and his contemporaries to start creating digital drawings was in its infancy at the dawn of the eighties. Apple, today widely regarded as the computer for creatives, had been set up in 1976 in California, but was yet to have an impact in the design world. However, in 1984, Apple announced the release of the first Macintosh range through its cinematic commercial "1984," directed by Ridley Scott. Only ever aired once, and that during the US Super Bowl, it immediately positioned Apple, with its advertising slogan: "the computer for the rest of us." With striking footage of a female athlete smashing a screen image of Big Brother, this stylish and emotive commercial helped Apple to play its own part in defining the visual esthetic of the decade. More importantly though, Apple had introduced the technology that would change the face of graphic design and image-making.

The Birth of Photoshop
It took a full three years for the Mac II, with the first color monitor, capable of displaying an impressive 256 colors. It took a further three years before the appearance of an early version of Photoshop, created for Adobe by brothers Thomas and John Knoll, following developments in the application that had originally started life as ImagePro. Photoshop's dominance had begun.

11

12

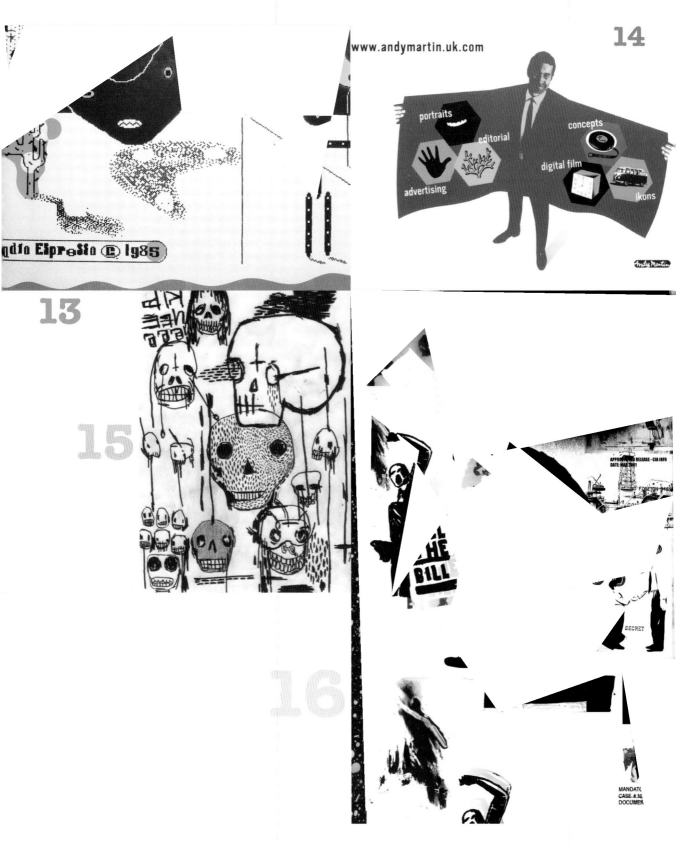

www.andymartin.uk.com

18

19

20

From the mid- to late eighties, designers and artists wishing to delve into digital practice faced numerous problems: the price of hardware was prohibitive, software was still complicated to use, and its functions were basic at best. Financial considerations ensured that the introduction of the digital into everyday working practices began in medium- to large-scale graphic design companies, but most small studios and freelance individuals did not have the capital for the set-up costs. This had a direct effect on the relationship that graphic design had with image-makers, who were predominantly solo or working within self-managed studio environments. In short, it was graphic design rather than image-making that took the lead. In 1992, John Warwicker, of design collective Tomato, said, "I can envisage a time when we'll all need our own individual Macs." Rewind just a short time and the digital world was a very different place from the one in which we live today.

Laser Light
Gradually, despite early difficulties, image-makers started to gain access to a new tool, one that would slowly introduce them to the notion of creating digital images. The Canon CLC, a color laser copier, provided the link between analog and digital methods of image creation for many. Early adopters of the CLC could resize originals, distort their shape, alter colors, create positives and negatives, and utilize an unprecedented range of image-manipulation tools. Andrew Coningsby, the man behind the illustration agency Debut Art, with offices in London, New York, Amsterdam, Frankfurt, and Sydney, recognized that a movement was beginning to evolve. "There was a move toward collage. With the CLC copying at £3.00 [c. US $5.50] a throw, a new direction was taking place. When you consider a basic set-up of computer, monitor, scanner, and printer was around £10,000 [c. US $18,200], it was hardly surprising that most illustrators stuck with the CLC for some time."

Meanwhile, alongside developments in digital technology, editorial design within the style press had started to evolve, taking on a more digital look. With the appointment of Neville Brody as Art Director at *The Face*, a bold new graphic language was developing. The introduction of the Mac sparked a revolution in publishing, with the ease of designing on-screen relegating paste-up design and production to the trash can. Within a few short years, the entire industry would be on board. For designers and art directors, increasingly aware of digital means of creation and reproduction, it was clear that those supplying the magazines with images would, at some point, have to fit into the digital loop.

The Impact of 128K RAM
Andy Martin left his job as Art Editor at *New Musical Express* to join the revolution. "I'd been laying out covers with pictures of cheesy mid-eighties bands and then quit in '85 as I could sense that something big was going to happen." Martin was introduced to the Mac a year before, by a key figure within Apple, when he was given a Mac with 128K of RAM to "play with, experiment with, and just see what I could do," he explains. "I was taken down to the PR office and was given the kit. It would have cost me an arm and a leg, and they just said 'take it.' How cool was that?" The impact on Martin's work was immense. He started to create digital illustrations for a variety of publications, all of which wanted to further their links with the changes in image creation that they knew were taking place.

With key figures like Wright and Martin in the UK, and John Hersey and J. Otto Seibold in the US making names for themselves by creating graphic images that went far beyond the boundaries of traditional illustration, others were starting to take notice. Publications willing to take risks with their visual approach gave new forms of image-making a platform, enabling other image-makers to follow their lead.

22. Paul Reilly, Topman/The Void, Kim Jones' collection launch
23. Miles Donovan, Tango/HHCL/*The Face* magazine cover, DeFace The Face
24. Jim Stoten, Gomez, *Silence* album sleeve

Profiles and Platforms

The most recent influx of digital image-making at *The Face* came when Graham Rounthwaite, having graduated with an MA in Illustration from the Royal College of Art in London, made the move from illustration image-making to design and art direction. Taking up the post of Art Editor at *The Face*, having worked on high-profile campaigns for Levi's as an illustrator in the late nineties, Rounthwaite began to make ripples. Despite enthusiasm for digital methods of working, it had taken almost a decade for a generation with the attitude and digital skills to match to emerge. Rounthwaite picked up on a small group of new image-makers, giving them creative freedom to produce innovative new work for the magazine. Jasper Goodall, Bump, and NEW were among this select group. It was through their work for *The Face* that offers of more lucrative projects for bigger clients rolled in.

The Death of the Style Press

The influence that the style press had enjoyed during its late-eighties heyday returned in the late nineties to make an impact on digital image-making and its relationship with other sectors of the design industry. The testing ground that *The Face* provided for new forms of working and the role that it played in bringing new talent to light is only now starting to gain the recognition and respect that it deserves. It may be a case of too little to late, however: *The Face* finally closed its doors in 2004, a year short of its twenty-fifth birthday.

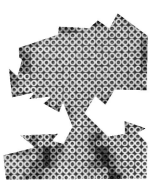

2

1

3

Ian Wright is the Daddy, maybe even the Granddaddy of contemporary illustration.

From Ian Wright's first job, at the end of the seventies, designing the cover of the Undertones' "Teenage Kicks" 7-inch single, to his frenetic weekly black-and-white portraits for *New Musical Express* in its eighties hey-day; from his in-your-face billboard campaign for Fosters Ice in the nineties, to his unique in-store installation for Issey Miyake in New York City in the noughties, Wright's work has spanned four decades. That is no small achievement.

Never one to stand still long enough to cash in on a creative approach, Wright has constantly forced his work into new directions. He has tested new developments in technology and mixed up techniques and materials, while creating unique visions that have remained in a constant flux.

Career Opportunities

Ian Wright never planned a career in illustration. Wright was working in a clerical job for the health service in Hoxton—before that part of East London was fashionable—when his colleagues, all women 30 years older, persuaded him to go to art school. A year of evening classes, another on an art and design foundation course, and three sharing a desk with Neville Brody at the London College of Printing, saw Wright enter the industry just as punk rock became new wave.

1. Personal project, Larry Levan
2. *Q* magazine, REM
3. Issey Miyake, Ghost Gorilla in progress

In May 1980, *The Face* launched its first-ever issue and Wright's work featured within. Featuring fashion, style, and music mixed together with contemporary design, *The Face* was the perfect outlet for Wright's fresh approach to image-making. His work, years later, bears very little resemblance to those early manic drawings, but the spirit within the work is still visible. Wright's use of materials has changed from job to job throughout his career. He has created images using just about anything that has come to hand. An early portrait of Grandmaster Flash saw Wright work entirely with salt to replicate cocaine as a reference to the seminal rap track "White Lines." Wright adopted photocopiers at an early stage, creating images by changing single color toners within the machine to mimic the screen-print process. He built layers of color from separate artworks into one final image. Working independently within Neville Brody's studio for many years, allowed Wright the luxury of dabbling with early Apple Macs. His choice of software in the early nineties was MacPaint, a funky little application created, as the name implies, for kids.

Portraits of the Artist
Portraits of Mike Tyson, Bjork, Ian Brown, Pete Townshend (the list goes on) for record sleeves and the music press, have allowed Wright to slip effortlessly between the analog and the digital. Wright is currently creating a portrait of civil rights campaigner Angela Davis, from 1,000 mascara brushes for *Black Book* magazine in the US. He is also creating a portrait of Henry Wellcome for The British Museum made entirely from reflective dots.

Wright commands huge respect for his leftfield approach to image-making, and it is not likely that his inventiveness will ever be tamed. Would-be illustrators and designers often approach Wright at his studio in East London for advice. Simple, he says: "Keep The Faith!"

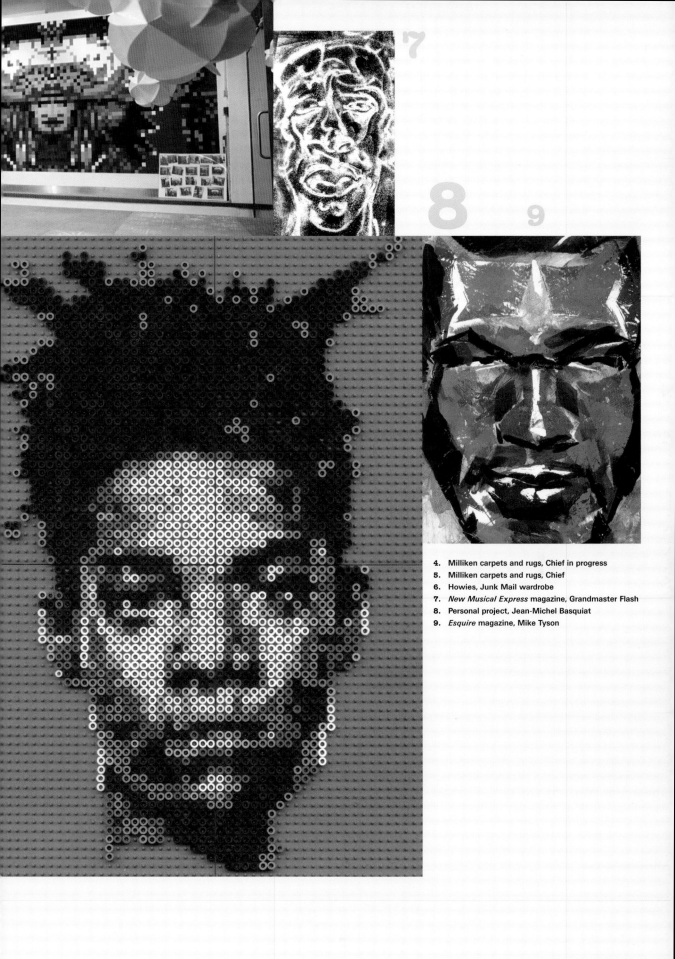

4. Milliken carpets and rugs, Chief in progress
5. Milliken carpets and rugs, Chief
6. Howies, Junk Mail wardrobe
7. *New Musical Express* magazine, Grandmaster Flash
8. Personal project, Jean-Michel Basquiat
9. *Esquire* magazine, Mike Tyson

1

3

California dreaming: this image-maker goes from "acoustic" painting to making digital pop art in the sun.

California's year-round sunshine should be the ideal place to grow outdoors—after all, the state's symbols include the giant redwood tree and the golden poppy. Michael Gillette's studio faces out on his small back yard, wooden decked and adorned with potted plants that, he admits "need some help." Gardening is not Gillette's thing.

Untitled

Making images, however, is. From the moment he won a book token as first prize in a school art competition—for his first major piece, *Untitled*—he was hooked. "From then on, it was the only road for me," he explains. "Well, I did want to join The Beatles, but that gig was long gone." Gillette admits to more than a passing interest in music. Two weeks out of college, in 1992, he won his first commission for the band St. Etienne, creating portraits of the group's members. This exposure saw Gillette pick up regular work for monthly music magazine *Select*, in London. His first job was to create images for a piece that

1. **Birth of Dub**, personal project
2. **The Five Boroughs**, The Beastie Boys, Web site
3. **Stereowolf**, T-Shirt

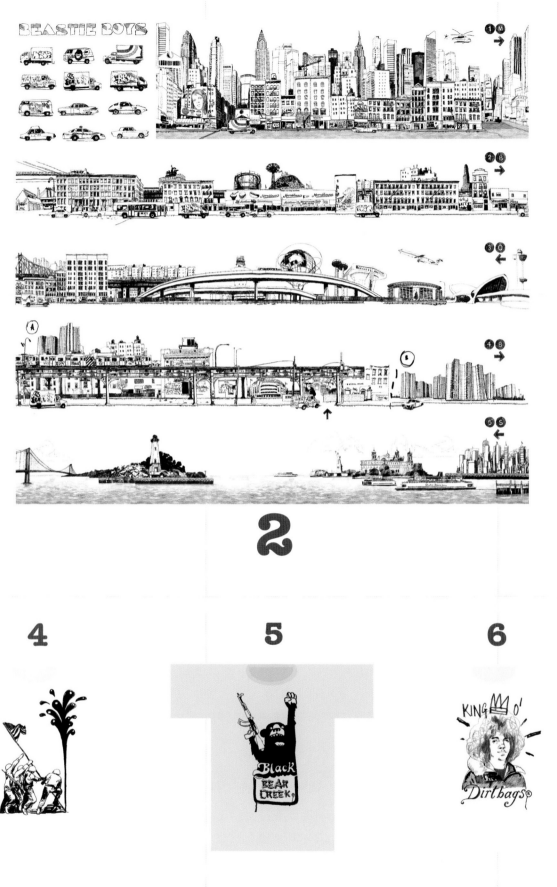

4. Oil War, T-Shirt
5. Black Bear Creek, T-Shirt
6. King Mo Dirtbags, T-Shirt

ushered in Britpop. Over the next six years, while he was based in London, Gillette worked on numerous projects and commissions that included diversions into pop promos for Britpop band Elastica.

While watching paint dry in 1999, Gillette decided that "it was time to embrace the digital revolution." Exhibiting his last "acoustic" works in Soho's trendy watering hole The Groucho Club was a landmark in his career. Gillette soon realized that being digital meant he could be almost anywhere on the planet. His decision to up and leave London for San Francisco in 2002 was inspired by a trip to the city back in 1997. "It's a truly unique place, small enough to be intimate with, but big enough to warrant a truly gigantic record store," explains Gillette, quickly referencing the city back to his love of music. "It's on the coast, the weather is great, and it's foxy pretty."

Inspirations

Reflecting on the artists and designers who have inspired his work, Gillette admits that music, not surprisingly, has played a huge part. "I'm obviously a big pop art fan, possibly because it was so connected to music," he states. He is also a fan of New York–based Pushpin Studios, whose work by founders Seymour Chwast and Milton Glaser made a phenomenal impact on design from the fifties though to the eighties. "Those Pushpin folk could draw like God," he states. "The most recent artist whose work really made me want to weep is Roger Andersson." Andersson, a Swedish watercolor artist, published a book of paintings in 2004—*Letters from Mayhem*. The simplicity and beauty of his work echoes Gillette's curve-ball take on popular culture.

Organic Processes

Gillette's projects start in a simple manner. "I read the brief, mull it over, and think up an idea, research it, look stuff up on the Internet, draw/paint the elements I think I need, scan them, and start fiddling around" is his honest description of his working process. "Generally, during this process, I decide on a better idea and redraw elements to fit," he explains. "It's quite organic." Gillette's gardening skills can't be described in the same way…

7.   Tommy Shots, *Young Heart Attack* sleeve design
8.   Ban Criminally Logged Timber, Greenpeace poster

1. *Surface* magazine, Adobe Software promotion
2. Big Active, Gogo digital print

Dark, moody, raw, and sexual best describe Jasper Goodall's influences and subject matter.

"A mag from Japan called *Tattoo Burst*, a book of erotic Chinese art, an incredible Korean book that categorizes thousands of animals and gives 50 different stylized representations of each of them …" Jasper Goodall is describing his desk top in his studio. He continues, "… loads of empty tea and coffee cups, bills I haven't paid, bits of paper with my drawings on them, and, oh yes, all my computer shit."

The fact that Goodall's choice of kit, including a high-end Mac running Photoshop and FreeHand, a Wacom tablet, scanner, and all manner of digital devices, seems to excite him far less than his felt-tips, pop-a-point pencils, crayons, and his wealth of global visual reference materials is an indication of how this image-maker approaches his creative work.

Creative Control

Goodall draws upon a range of interests, including a sojourn in Japan for training in martial arts. He has become pretty adept at creating fashion-based but gutsy images as part of major advertising campaigns for a range of clients, including Levi's and Nike. It is, however, his work for defunct style magazine *The Face* that always excited him most, as creative control remained firmly within his own grasp. "I hate clients who dictate. I once worked on a very big project for a stressed art director who slammed the phone down on me, so we only communicated via e-mail. One e-mail, demanding changes to my artwork, angered me so much that I spat at his message on my screen!"

Angry Young Man

Goodall is obviously prepared to stand by his principles; he once attacked a UK national newspaper, *The Observer*, for making changes to one of his images, removing a semierect penis without his permission. Leading monthly design publication *Creative Review* ran a two-page feature on the fiasco, looking in depth at issues of digital manipulation and ownership of copyright after Goodall made them aware of his treatment at the hands of the newspaper. "The best thing about working as a freelance illustrator must be the freedom," explains Goodall, "but the worst thing has to be the number of talentless art directors who desire control!"

Dark and Dirty

Sex remains at the forefront of the subject matter explored within Goodall's work. He cites pornography, along with eighties' singer Gary Numan and US author Bret Easton Ellis, as influences. This goes some way to explaining his visual take on the subject. His images are littered with fashionable and beautiful, sometimes vacant, other times powerful-looking women, with an undercurrent of a much darker, moodier place. It seems fitting that Goodall has just completed another fashion range; his second line of bikinis, the first in conjunction with his agent, Big Active, launched at a fashionable gallery in West London. Goodall's 2-D digital fashion world meets the real world in 3-D form, harnessing the same snarly attitude as that captured within his illustrations.

3. Personal project, Crows
4. Bikini range, Jolly Roger
5. *The Face* magazine, Commune

NEW's iconic image of English soccer star David Beckham graces the cover of <u>The Guardian</u> newspaper's weekly listings magazine, <u>The guide</u>.

Austin Cowdell and Matt Hamilton at NEW were commissioned to create a cover for *The guide* magazine that gave a street-style coolness to David Beckham, a soccer and fashion icon. The accompanying article investigated and celebrated the birth of punk rock, looking at why the movement was so important, but how apathy had set in among the nation's youth.

NEW's graphic language adopts both the visual esthetic of street graffiti and the lurid technocolors of the punk rock movement. Working with techniques that incorporate both traditional and digital processes, they set about creating an image that typifies and illustrates the headline "Apathy in the UK." Beckham is transformed from a glossy pinup to a gritty, urban, moody graphic as NEW bring their image-making skills to bear.

1 NEW scour photo libraries and Web sites for a bold image of David Beckham, and start to test out their approach to a number of these found images. Here a photographic portrait is scanned at A4 size (8¹⁄₈ x 11¹¹⁄₁₆in/210 x 297mm), at 300dpi.

2 In Photoshop, the scan is accurately cleaned up; all minor defects in the scan are fixed and the image is touched up to remove blemishes. The brightness and contrast are increased and the file is saved as a TIFF.

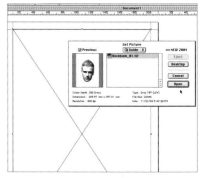

3 The TIFF is saved as a grayscale image and imported into QuarkXPress. A page layout application such as InDesign could also be used.

4 The image is then printed at 300dpi onto A4 paper using a simple black-and-white printout from a color ink-jet.

5 Using the printout as the canvas, the shadows within the image are converted into continuous line using handrendered drawing techniques. The paper-based image is then scanned back into Photoshop.

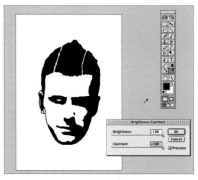

6 Once again, the brightness and contrast are adjusted to the maximum setting and the file is saved as a TIFF.

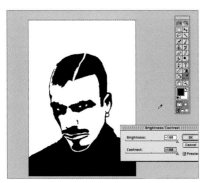

7 NEW work with numerous images of Beckham, taking each one to the same stage, before making their final choice of image for the piece.

8 The chosen image is printed out and converted into a stencil, while decisions about the colors are made. Deciding on a palette of colors, and where each will best work, is integral to a successful solution.

9 Although the final image has the appearance of having been stenciled directly onto a wall, neatly echoing urban street art and graffiti, it has actually been created on specially prepared, handpainted, textured paper.

10 The stencil is taped into place to avoid any movement, and sprayed using industrial spray paints. The mix of colors and layers, having been carefully selected, are added in the relevant sequence.

11 As the final cover lines for the magazine need to look as integral to the image as possible, NEW create headlines in the typographic style of the magazine and recreate logos.

12 Employing a technique that ages and distorts graphics—scanning, printing, photocopying, and rescanning—the type treatments are given the punk esthetic.

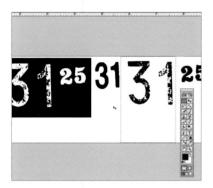

13 Numerals are created for the issue's date in the same way, and all chosen elements are imported into the final image.

14 There are no set rules at this stage. NEW work with the visual elements that they have created to start playing with the composition. Constant slight adjustments are made until they are happy with exactly how the image is starting to look.

15 Even at this stage, experimentation continues as other colorways are explored before final creative decisions are made. Once all has been completed, the image is delivered to *The Guardian* as an e-mail attachment.

16 In print and in situ, the image is studied carefully by NEW to gauge how the printing process has translated their work. An image will always appear slightly different in print than on screen as the way a monitor creates color is very different from how print works.

1

1. Boys Will Never Die, promotional project
2. John Peel, *Dazed & Confused* magazine
3. Welcome To The Brave New World, John Brown Citrus Publishing, article

2

3

2

Mixing Media & Techniques

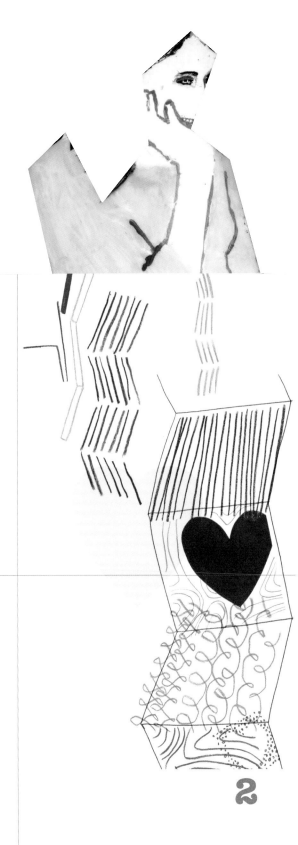

Risk-taking and an appreciation of accidental mistakes, combined with a solid underpinning in the language of creativity, leads to new forms of image-making.

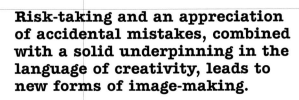

In 1973, Luke Rhinehart wrote and published a novel that has remained a permanent fixture in student apartments throughout the US and Europe. *The Dice Man* is the story of a psychiatrist, locked into a life of order and routine, who decides to let the roll of the dice govern his every decision. This intriguing story captured, and continues to capture, the imagination of a youth yet to fully comprehend how to live their lives, how to navigate and negotiate the complexities of day-to-day living. More importantly, as well as appearing to offer an alternative route through the mainstream and mundane existence led by the majority of the population, the book forced a view of risk-taking and chance as a glamorous and exciting lifestyle choice. Despite rarely appearing on book lists for art and design students—most art schools opt for books on theory and practice rather than literature—the attitude and mindset of the novel impresses those with an artistic and creative viewpoint: the importance of risk-taking within creative image-making has so often been overlooked.

Perfect Platforms
Ensuring that the conditions within art and design education are conducive to taking creative risks is just part of the problem that has faced art schools for many years. While design education recognizes the benefits of making and learning from mistakes, of being unfazed by traversing new routes in order to produce exciting and challenging visual solutions, it is often criticized for being too unaware of commercial realities and constraints. Creating a perfect platform, available at the right price, and accessible to the right number of students, has never been a simple task. The modern-day "solution" owes much to an approach that was born in Germany early in the twentieth century.

1. Ceri Amphlett, personal project, Maybe
2. Jenny Bowers, Penguin Books, catalog introduction
3. Supergympie, *Studio* magazine, Killer Technique
4. Mr. Bingo, personal project, I Had Sex With My Own Ass In Front Of My Dog
5. Andy Martin, Department for International Development, The Granary

Building House

The Bauhaus design school was founded in Weimar in 1919. Although initially concerned with the teaching of architecture (Bauhaus is German for "building house"), it attempted to create a new unison between art and industry. The Bauhaus approach revolutionized the teaching of art and design, and its influence can still be felt throughout Europe, the US, and even Japan. Underpinning the Bauhaus ethos was the fact that artists, designers, and craftspeople worked together to create the removal of conventional subject barriers. Students studied a variety of disciplines, with initial lecture-based study followed by hands-on training in workshops. Subjects included the study of nature, fabrics, materials and tools, geometry, color and composition, and construction and presentation. Students undertook classes across a range of disciplines including drawing, painting, sculpture, photography, typography, advertising, furniture design, and interior design. Through the teachings of such eminent artists and designers as Johannes Itten, Walter Gropius, Herbert Bayer, Wassily Kandinsky, Laszlo Moholy-Nagy, and Paul Klee, students of the Bauhaus school were taught, in the words of its manifesto, "the only thing that can be learned; the language of creativity." The mix and marriage of materials that this encouraged, together with the breaking down of boundaries between artists and craftspeople, produced a unique foundation stone for today's education of the artist/designer.

Shock of the New

Nearly a century after the introduction of this Bauhaus method of art education, and several decades on from the risk-taking proposals put forward by Rhinehart in *The Dice Man*, it would appear that these two seemingly unassociated events have both played a part in the development of recent movements in creative image-making. It is the mix of media and materials, along with the element of surprise and risk, that motivates many of the people working in digital image-making today.

In the mid-seventies, a documentary series on modern art, and its accompanying book, used the title "The Shock of the New." This reflected the view of modern art held by the general public at the time, and

fitted the program brilliantly. It is also an apt description of the effect that digital technology had on the fairly safe and secure world of illustration when it was unleashed toward the end of the following decade. While the forward-thinking, fashion-conscious graphic design world grappled with digital technology from the earliest opportunity, illustration kept much of the hardware, software, and new working methods at arm's length. The humble illustrator wanted nothing to do with the digital, preferring older, traditional, and more established ways of working. Unlike the innovative Bauhaus approach to materials and methods, most illustrators followed entrenched practices; it took some time for digital technology to break into and change their working methodology.

11

12

13

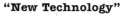

"New Technology"

On reflection, it is clear that the illustrator/image-makers' preoccupation with and love for traditional methods has played a huge part in the recent combination of tried and tested techniques with digital technology. "New" technology once meant digital technology, but as more and more art students grow up with access to computers, this description is no longer appropriate. For many of these students, the "traditional" techniques and methods could more accurately be described as "new."

Old-School Art

Art and design education, at its best, still introduces students to many forms of artistic expression through a range of disciplines that includes etching, lithography, and screen printing; black-and-white photography and darkroom processing; analog animation; and bookbinding, letterpress, and woodblock printing. Students learn how to improve their drawing skills through observational and interpretative drawing in the studio and life class; they are taught theories and principles of color, layout, type, and image; and are given a full grounding in the history of their discipline. The combination of this practical, theoretical, and cultural underpinning of the subject with digital technology has opened up a range of working methods that are defining a new visual esthetic. The super-realistic, close-to-perfection results that first appeared when image-editing applications, such as Photoshop, were launched, and the clean-edge, mechanical drawing techniques employed by users of Illustrator and FreeHand have started to fade into the background as a more "messed-up" esthetic has emerged.

Graduates often discover that recreating the art school studio is an expensive endeavor, but financial requirements do shrink annually. The normal host of input devices has not varied dramatically from year to year—the mouse, keyboard, and scanner have been around a while, and other devices have become less expensive. Graphics tablets, digital cameras, and digital camcorders are all cases in point. Much of the most interesting work being created today utilizes older techniques within modern technology to create genuinely new working practices.

14

15

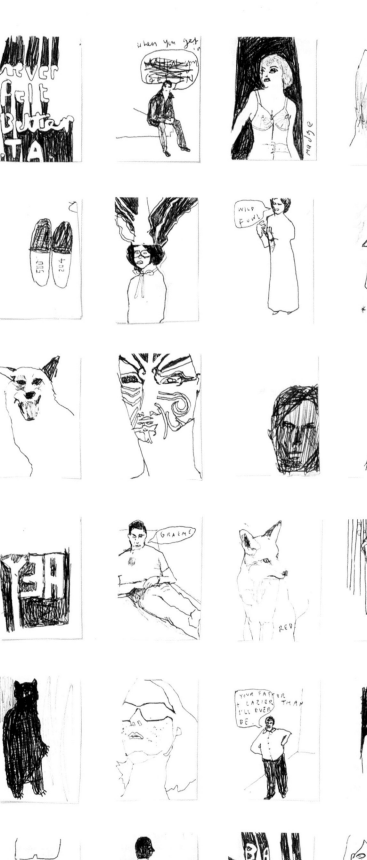
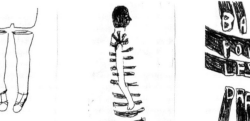

17

18

Make Mistakes

The casual mistake of misregistration, the overprint of one color, the odd bleed of another, the drip of a paint mixed a little too wet, or the slight sticking of ink in the mesh of a silk screen are all accidents that may take a visual image in a new direction. It is often the case that "things going wrong" can dictate new directions in work; recreating these accidents using digital means, although entirely possible, requires firsthand experience of working with traditional materials and methods. Composing an image of painterly textures, creating layers using hand-drawn elements, adding swirls and swishes of real-time and real-life color can imbue it with a timeless depth.

The journey through education and practice into creating a unique and personal visual language or working style is a complex one. Staying ahead of the game, constantly mixing techniques and creating new working methods to keep one step ahead of the copyists is never an easy task, but experimentation with materials, risk-taking, and stepping into the unknown provides the most conducive environment for change and for new work to be created.

16. Ceri Amphlett, Parker Pens/Pentagram, Ballpoint Fiftieth Anniversary
17. Chrissie Macdonald, self-published book, *Woodland*
18. Lee Ford, personal project, Too Many Cooks ...

16

19

20

19. Lucy Vigrass, *Saturday Telegraph Magazine*, Rita Konig column
20. Neasden Control Centre, *Stereo Type Magazine*, cover image

50 Section One: Working Process

I'M NO GOOD

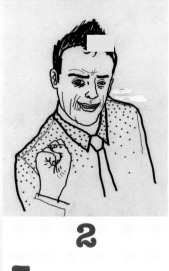

1

2

Dubious drawings, impending gloom, and bits of flotsam—a desktop in East London.

"A few years ago, during the World Cup [soccer] Finals," Paul Davis recounts, "I called a client to say I was ill and needed a few more days to finish a job. At the same time, I clumsily moved on the sofa, sitting on the remote control. The volume increased dramatically and the client heard 'and that's a beautiful goal from Ronaldo!' Needless to say, I lost the job." As well as his legendary love of soccer, Davis is also a big fan of at least two London private drinking clubs, claiming the award, in his own words, "Drinker of the Year—ask any landlord." In reality, Davis has picked up awards from *Creative Review* magazine; been named as Cartoonist of the Year, as voted for by journalists; and has work featured regularly in the D&AD annual collection of award-winning design.

Instantly recognizable, Davis' wry takes on fashionable East London types have been spotted across the pages of various magazines and newspapers, including *Dazed and Confused*, *Time Out*, and *The Independent*. In fact, it is an eight-page fashion feature for *The Independent on Sunday* magazine, commissioned by Art Director Jo Dale in 1997, that Davis attributes to being a career-defining moment. "The phone hasn't stopped ringing since that job, thanks to Jo," says Davis.

3

FAKE LONDON GENIUS

FUTUREMET +39 0283 900 192
FOURWORKS +44 20 7251 6180

1. I'm No Good, personal project
2. I'm Brilliant, personal project
3. FAKE London Genius poster

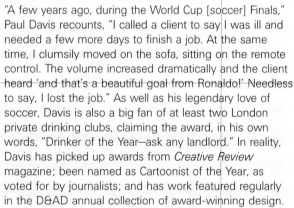

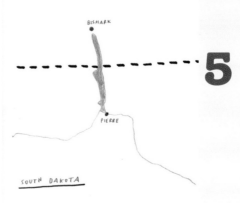

Paris, Tokyo, Stockholm, New York

Recently, that phone has also rung from clients all around the globe. "I've worked on a cookbook for a Canadian publisher, a series of images for an exhibition in Paris, a set of prints for a gallery in Tokyo, and a calendar for Save The Children in Stockholm," Davis casually admits. He has also had a couple of books published recently, including one of his unpublished work and another on how Americans and Britons view each other. Davis toured the US researching, drawing, and speaking to people as he traveled, recording their thoughts and opinions.

Digital Documentation

Davis has adopted digital technology purely as a means to document, archive, market, and distribute his work. When describing his working environment, he says very little about his choice of hardware. In fact, he dryly lists the following items as taking pride of place on his desk: "a computer, a cup of tea, a pile of papers I'm too scared to look at, external hard drive, bits of flotsam, scanner, dubious drawings, impending gloom, video camera, mouse, dodgy erotica." The surface of the desk may describe more the Davis state of mind than any working process.

Capturing the Moment

Many of Davis' drawings are done on the move. He works in small sketchbooks, capturing conversations, moments, and moods which are then translated into final pieces back in his studio. Quick sketches, doodles, drawings, and observations are a vital part of the Davis working method. He once exhibited 3,000 drawings on Post-its at the Dazed and Confused Gallery in London. Davis' continued hard work and determination have paid off. He has come a very long way since his first commission for the long-dead listings magazine *City Limits*; "I got paid 12 quid. Honest!" The Paul Davis World Cup "honesty" springs to mind once again.

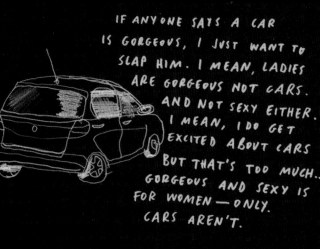

IF ANYONE SAYS A CAR IS GORGEOUS, I JUST WANT TO SLAP HIM. I MEAN, LADIES ARE GORGEOUS NOT CARS. AND NOT SEXY EITHER. I MEAN, I DO GET EXCITED ABOUT CARS BUT THAT'S TOO MUCH.. GORGEOUS AND SEXY IS FOR WOMEN — ONLY. CARS AREN'T.

6

CECI N'EST PAS MICROSOFT

DAVIS

7

8

FAKE LONDON GENIUS

INFORMATION: FOURMARKETING +44 20 7287 8767

9

10

FAKE LONDON GENIUS

FUTURENET +39 0289 900 198
FOURWORKS +44 20 7251 6180

JUBILANT

11

12

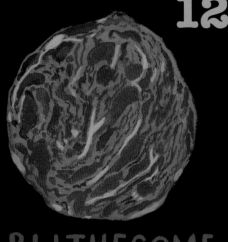

BLITHESOME

13

吉本新喜劇
N¥C ロンドン
88

DAVIS

14

Profile: Marion Deuchars

1

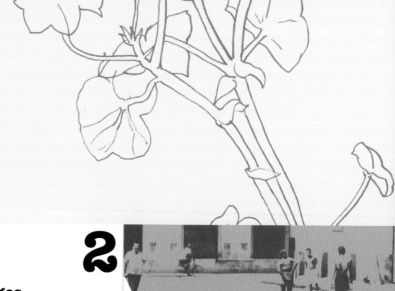

2

Research and development through play for Marion Deuchars' ever-evolving images.

"I have numerous incidents of missing artwork," recalls Marion Deuchars. "The best was a returned A2 painted illustration, folded carefully into quarters and squeezed into an A4 envelope. My mouth remained open, in shock, for some time afterwards. Luckily, nowadays most of my work is sent digitally."

Learning to Love the Digital
Deuchars learnt to love the computer early in her career. Prior to agency representation, she mailed out mini digital portfolios saved onto floppy disks, long before CD-ROMs were affordable. Work that began from scanning drawings and paintings, and later combined her digital photographs, presented well as a digital portfolio, in advance of most image-makers even considering this approach an option.

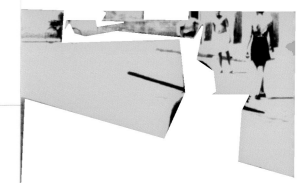

3

4

Computer, Desk, and Play Desk

Deuchars is one of a rare breed of image-makers who continue to adapt and push their work into new directions. It is her studio setup that enables this continued research and development. "I have two desks, one for the computer and one for playing on," she explains. "On the computer desk right now there is a G4, a Wacom tablet, a calculator, a Nikon Coolpix, a telephone, a diary, and a list of things to do." Deuchars makes an attempt to define the other desk. "My play desk is full of stuff; paints, paper, three large tubs of brushes in water (that have been there too long), four different plastic palettes, six different rolls of tape, tubes of gouache, a box of charcoal, various boxes of stencils … That's all I can see on the 'top layer' right now."

Working in illustration since graduating from the Royal College of Art, London, at the end of the eighties, Deuchars now teaches there and can count numerous working illustrators and image-makers as former students of hers.

Deuchars believes that getting out and meeting clients is the best way to generate commissions when first starting out. "Agents are not a good idea at first. It is important to 'pound the boards' and meet and understand one's own industry personally," she explains. "Some of my original contacts are people I still work with and have a good relationship with."

Bonus

Deuchars has picked up a Creative Futures Award, membership of the prestigious Alliance Graphique International (AGI), and an enviable client list. Deuchars is in demand. Her current ongoing projects include three book jacket designs, a chair design for a company in Helsinki, color studies for the Cricket Building in Derby, England, and 15 portraits for *Wallpaper** magazine. She would have it no other way. "I like making images; being paid for it is a bonus."

5

1. Untitled, Planeta catalog image
2. Baseball, personal project
3. Les Cazuelas, Spain, personal project
4. Picture This, British Council poster
5. Cuba, personal project

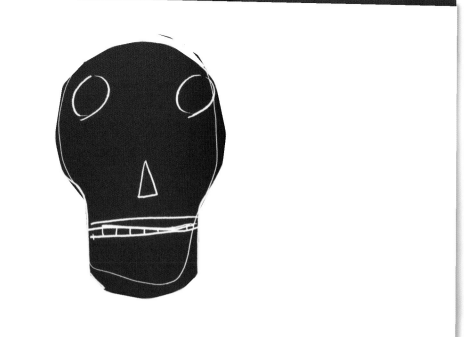

AUTOBIOGRAFÍA

Las palabras
JEAN-PAUL SARTRE

LOSADA

6

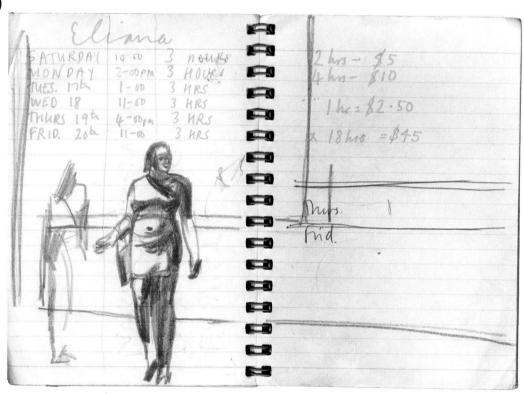

8

6. Untitled, 4th Estate catalog image
7. *Las palabras*, book jacket
8. Untitled sketchbook image, personal project

2

1

1. *Deadly Kin* book jacket
2. Euryanthe, *The Independent* newspaper, short story
3. Juice Detox, *The Independent* newspaper, feature

3

IT specialist required for busy ex-print-maker...

"In my precomputer days I worked using relief printing, a very long-winded process that often meant all-night sessions in the studio to meet deadlines," explains Shonagh Rae who shares Studio 100 with around 20 designers, architects, and other illustrators. "Occasionally," she elaborates, "I would have to courier work that was still drying. One time when I got a copy of the magazine that an illustration appeared in, I realized that the artwork had completely stuck to the inside of the envelope in transit. The art director had made a vague attempt at peeling it off, but it had gone to print anyway! I booked to go on a Photoshop course the next day."

Image-maker and IT specialist

That early lesson was a tough one, but it changed the course of Rae's work in a way she could not have imagined. Currently one of the busiest image-makers in the editorial and publishing fields, Rae has successfully developed her time-consuming, labor-intensive print techniques into a digital process that echoes her earlier work, evoking much of its texture and richness, while never needing hours to dry. For Rae, though, the digital comes with another set of problems. "One of the worst things about what I do is having to be my own IT specialist," she explains.

4

4. Crimea, *Highlife Magazine*, feature
5. *Powder Monkey* book jacket
6. Genetic Sexual Attraction, *The Guardian* newspaper, article
7. London Wine Fair, *Highlife Magazine*, feature

The fact that Rae is currently working on numerous projects means that she may well be on the way to employing her own IT professional. "I'm working on a piece for *MAMM* magazine—an American publication for women suffering from breast cancer—three book jackets for novelist Jake Arnott, another for a new author, Louise Dean, images for *New Scientist* magazine, others for an annual company report, and some editorial stuff," lists Rae. Represented by the leading contemporary illustration agency Heart, Rae understands the value of having an agent to assist in managing the financial aspects of the job. "I decided to work through an agent as, like a lot of flimsy illustrators, I don't like the messy business of talking money."

Personal Vision

Rae is very happy with her current studio setup, but the route to joining Studio 100 was not straightforward. "My first studio was above Burger King in Camden Town, and in the years since it seems like I have shared a studio with pretty much every illustrator and image-maker in London," she explains. Rae's approach to her work, her journey from print studio to computer screen via numerous studios, is echoed in the advice she gives to those just starting out. "Develop a personal way of working and then decide where you might fit into illustration, rather than the other way around." The IT skills can be picked up on the way.

5

6

7

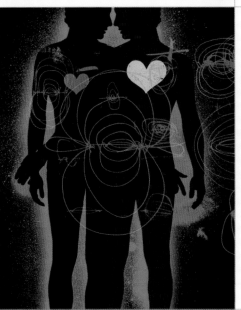

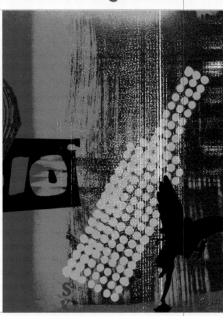

Tutorial 2: Steve Wilson

A cutting-edge mix of old and new technology merges to create organized chaos in Steve Wilson's graphic image of Selfish C**t.

Understanding how to bring art-school energy to an image can stretch both analog and digital abilities to the full. To create this image for *The Observer Music Monthly*, Steve Wilson started by working from an original photograph supplied by the band's PR company. With little reference material, and a tight deadline to meet, Wilson created this iconic image by seamlessly merging various working processes together.

Using hand-cut paper, card stencils, and spray paint alongside classic Photoshop techniques, Wilson operated both inside and outside the computer to create this strikingly visual image. Here, we look in detail at the step-by-step decisions taken and the full working process that led to the final solution, execution, and production of this arresting image.

1 This is the original photograph, by Andrew Kendall, supplied by the PR company as reference material.

2 In Photoshop, the image contrast is adjusted to the maximum and the brightness made as strong tonally as possible. The trick is to enhance details and shadows within the image.

3 Here the image is cut out using paths in Photoshop, and select areas have their edges smoothed off using the filter Dust and Scratch. Areas requiring more detail are redrawn.

4 The image is broken down with the Wand Tool into three separate color layers, filling in total areas so that each color overlays in the right order—yellow, red, then black. These three colors are used in this order to gain the most contrast.

5 Each of the color separations is then converted into black to ease the process of hand-cutting stencils. They are then printed out onto A4 sheets using an ink-jet printer.

6 Each printout is enlarged onto an A3 sheet (11¾ x 16½in/297 x 420mm) using a photocopier: this keeps the detail in the image and aids the cutting of the stencil as the line work is far more visible.

7 Cutting stencils takes care and time. One mistake and the process must be started over again. Using a cutting mat and a sharp blade is essential.

8 Using regular car spray paints, each stencil is sprayed through to create individual images on separate sheets of paper.

9 Care is taken to make the image look sprayed: the desired effect is that of a hastily drawn, cut, and sprayed image, despite the lengthy process this actually requires.

10 Each of the sheets is then reduced back to A4 (8⅛ x 11¹¹⁄₁₆in/210 x 297mm) using a photocopier. This tightens up the image and ensures easy scanning on an inexpensive A4 flatbed scanner.

11 Back in Photoshop, each scan is converted into a single color once again. In effect, the stenciled version is now back in the computer.

12 The three scans are then repositioned in Photoshop, with each layer placed in the correct order, as shown.

13 A series of new marks are made using the spray can. These looser marks are more free-form than can be created using tools within the software.

14 Each of the marks is scanned into Photoshop and placed into the document; they are used to add extra texture within the image.

15 Free-form paint-drip marks are added to the base image. Small effects like this give the impression that the entire image was created using nondigital techniques. Added "realism" can make all the difference to the final image.

16 Here extra work on the blue layer is undertaken. An added paint effect is used to cover areas that have been cut away. This is done simply by using the Lasso Tool and deleting selected areas. The added textures cover the sharp cut lines to ensure that the image retains the sprayed effect.

17 At this stage the blue and pink/purple layers are overlaid—the hand and wrist is connected to the arm. To ensure a correct fit, the images are scaled to the same relative size.

18 Elements of the yellow scan are removed using the Lasso Tool, and prescanned drips are added to create a greater overall balance.

19 Each of the layers is checked and repositioned, all the while referring back to the original photo. Small extras—a wristband—are added at this stage where the image needs further detailing.

20 The hand and wrist require more prominence in the image. Vector-drawn paths from Illustrator are created, filled with green, and added to give weight and extra solidity.

21 The final image (which could be saved as a TIFF or a JPEG), is e-mailed to the art department at the magazine and within days—this is a weekly newspaper supplement after all—the issue appears on the newsstands.

1

2

3

4

1. Pearcestoner Associates Ltd., compliments slips and post-outs
2. Reggae fashion image, *Jalouse* magazine, fashion feature (photo by Joe Lacey)
3. Totem, promotional project
4. Garden, Neiman Marcus department store, shopping bag

Revival,
Appropriation,
and Reuse

"Computers are to design as microwaves are to cooking," exclaimed legendary US graphic designer Milton Glaser.

At the time he made that comment, Glaser had a valid point. With the introduction of digital technology, much of the graphic design being created was essentially a reheated, re-served version of what had been made earlier, using traditional methods. Although there were a number of key individuals pushing the technology and creating entirely new ways of working—namely April Greiman in graphic design and John Hersey in illustration, both in the US—most of the work did not break any boundaries. Glaser, a prolific designer and illustrator, made his name with witty conceptual design solutions as part of Pushpin Studios in New York, which he cofounded with Seymour Chwast, in 1954. It was Glaser's concept-led approach to visual communication, rather than the traditional esthetic style, that ignited a new vision of graphic design at that time.

I ♥ Logos

When he designed the I♥NY logo for the New York State Department of Commerce in 1976, Glaser could not have foreseen just how much impact one piece of graphic design could have. Widely regarded as the most imitated design in the history of the logo, today it can be found anywhere and everywhere. From coffee cup to T-shirt, from bumper sticker to baseball cap, the logo has been reused and reinterpreted, and the idea reappropriated for all manner of uses. Most versions are a pale imitation of Glaser's logo, and while often claimed the sincerest form of flattery, imitation in this case has lessened and cheapened the impact of the original.

The simplicity of the design is the perfect mix of type and image. The heart symbol demonstrates the perfect use of an existing icon, typifying image-making based on the reuse of existing images, symbols, and signs—a mix-and-match approach that steadily gained momentum as it became technically easier and culturally more accepted.

CHILDREN ARE BORN
WITH THESE ARMS
NOT THESE ARMS

5

6

**OBJECTS OF
LIMITED VALUE**

VORBIRE
INTERZI
REGIUNA

7

8

5. Mr. Bingo, Oxfam, Children Are Born With These Arms
6. Anthony Burrill, personal project, Objects of Limited Value
7. Brian Cairns, Ridley Scott Associates Films, Jake Scott wedding invitation
8. David Foldvari, Stoique (Japan), Graffiti Meets Windows (live painting event)
9. Martin O'Neill, *Adweek* magazine, Modest Change
10. Faile, Pro-Ked, sneaker design

9

10

Digital Revolution

In 1975, the first computer to warrant serious attention—the MITS (Micro Instrumentation Telemetry Systems) Altair—went on sale. It required assembly and needed expansion cards to run the keyboard and monitor. Two thousand were sold at US $439 (c. £240) each. The following year, Apple made its debut with the Apple II, the first model being a short-lived experimental precursor. Unveiled at the first West Coast Computer Fair in San Francisco, Apple II boasted a built-in keyboard, an audiocassette drive for storage, and just 4KB of RAM. The Apple II retailed at US $1,298 (c. £700). The Commodore Pet was also launched in 1976, but perhaps bigger news, although not at the time, was the setting up of Microsoft in Albuquerque, New Mexico, by Bill Gates and Paul Allen. The digital revolution had begun, though it was yet to play a part in graphic design.

Model 914

One of the first pieces of equipment to play a role in defining the reuse of images was the humble office photocopier. Invented by Chester F. Carlson in 1937 and patented as Electric Photography in the US in 1942, it took a further 18 years to find a business that was interested in the technology. Finally, the Haloid Company brought Carlson's idea to market. A year after its successful launch of the first ever fully automated photocopier, the company changed its name to Xerox Corporation. Model 914 was named after the paper size it could handle—9 x 14in.

With the photocopier starting to make an appearance in offices during the sixties and, as prices came down, appearing in design companies, copy shops, and public libraries throughout the seventies, the ability to create inexpensive, technically straightforward, and graphically accurate copies proved a real asset for freelance designers and image-makers. No longer were expensive PMT (photomechanical transfer) machines needed to create black-and-white copies of original artwork: a one-person design/illustration company could produce similar results with a cheap photocopier. This new ease in reproduction led to a proliferation of graphics that reused existing images.

Cut-and-Paste

Cultural factors also played a part. In the mid-seventies, punk rock had a dramatic impact on graphic design. In New York, emerging through the clubs, it manifested itself predominantly through music, while in the UK the focus was broader, with music, fashion, graphics, and design all feeling its influence. The speed-fueled sound of punk required a graphic language that depicted a new raw energy as far removed visually as it was aurally from what came before. The do-it-yourself concept of punk was translated through the work of graphic artists and designers like Jamie Reid, for the Sex Pistols, and Malcolm Garrett, for the Buzzcocks.

DINERO

Jamie Reid created the ransom-note, cut-and-paste graphic language that later defined the look and feel of punk while he was designing *Suburban Press*, a radical political magazine that ran for five years from 1970. He created a range of subversive graphics and slogans that were printed onto stickers. These included "Save Petrol— Burn Cars" and "Keep Warm This Winter—Make Trouble." The use of cheap materials, the photocopier, black-and-white imagery, and ripped edges came to characterize punk. Malcolm McLaren, manager of the Sex Pistols, invited Reid to design graphics for the band while he and Vivienne Westwood created their own avenue for punk rebellion through the clothes they designed for their shop, Sex. T-shirts depicted cut-up swastikas, pornographic images, and Union Jacks in tatters. In true punk style, Reid reappropriated a portrait of the Queen, by Cecil Beaton, for the Sex Pistols' single "God Save the Queen." The Queen's portrait also appeared on T-shirts, with a safety pin piercing her lips. Reusing, reconfiguring, and reinterpreting, long before recycling became the norm, punk led a revolution in redefining the visuals of graphic design.

15

16

17

From Punk to Hip-Hop

When rap music emerged from the New York housing projects in the late seventies, it introduced the culture of reusing beats and sounds from existing records. One of the first rap recordings, "Rapper's Delight" by the Sugarhill Gang, was released in 1979. It utilized bass lines and beats from the disco track "Good Times," originally recorded by Chic. "Rapper's Delight" went on to become the biggest-selling 12-inch single in history, shifting more than two million copies around the globe and adding a word to the popular vocabulary—hip-hop is a lyric used in the song. Rap borrowed from gospel and jazz, soul, funk, and disco, and its characteristic remixing of beats from different sources became known as sampling. Associations and links between punk and hip-hop have often been commented on. Don Letts, a filmmaker and former punk DJ, recalls that "punk was a complete subculture. Nothing since then has been so complete. I still live by all that shit. Hip-hop is black punk rock."

Visual Sampling

Reusing images, icons, signs, and symbols has been part of image-making and graphic art for many years. As punk stole from the establishment and hip-hop sampled from existing musical genres, so Andy Warhol and pop art before them plundered popular visual culture. Marilyn Monroe, Campbell's soup cans, and Coca-Cola bottles were all up for grabs. Digital technology was not the instigator, but it has made aspects of the process easier; getting access to a cheap scanner to import "found" elements into a design is now a far simpler process than gaining access to a PMT camera or a photocopier was over 20 years ago.

Shifts in expectations, led by changes in how both music and design can be created, have given the visualizer a new creative freedom. Access to images has never been greater, whether through a 30-second Google image search or wandering around a flea market or garage sale picking up printed ephemera. There is always an image crying out to be reused and given new life.

18. Joe Magee, *New Scientist* magazine, DNA Palm Reading
19. Richard May, The Apartment, Under Construction party invite
20. NEW, *Time Out* magazine, The Money Trap: Criminal Cons with Student Loans

1

OBJECTS OF
LIMITED VALUE

2

SITOI KITU!

UMOJA
NI NGUVU

IF YOU SUSPECT ANY CORRUPTION PLEASE REPORT IT TO US AT:
KENYA ANTI-CORRUPTION COMMISSION
INTEGRITY CENTRE, MILIMANI / VALLEY RD. JUNCTION,
PO BOX 61130 NAIROBI
TEL: 2718812 / 2719553 FAX: 2719757 e-mail: kacc@integrity.go.ke

1. *Objects of Limited Value*, personal project, limited-edition book
2. Sitoi Kitu!, Kenyan Anti-Corruption Commission, poster

Engaging and amusing his audience are prime motives for this globe-trotting image-maker.

Travel plays a part in Anthony Burrill's search for inspiration. He enjoys the experience. "Seeing different places is exciting." The way things look and smell differently, he says, is what can effect changes in his work, "although it's not until you get back home that you can start to process all the new things you've seen. Then it starts to seep into the work quite subconsciously."

Enthusiast at Work

Burrill's work is quiet and unassuming, but has a presence and sense of humor that engages the viewer. "I'm very interested in things and I love finding out about new things," he states. "I like meeting new people and seeing how they approach their work. I think my work has a friendliness that engages with people. I don't load my work with layers of meaning—it's bright and cheerful. It's an extension of me. It's very simple too, like me."

3

WORK HARD & BE NICE TO PEOPLE

4

5

Engage and Amuse

There is a refreshing honesty to Burrill's frank admission of how his work communicates. There is nothing cool or ironic in his descriptions of the process; what you see is what you get. "I use lots of little phrases that I pick up in conversation. 'Work hard and be nice to people' was overheard at the checkout in a supermarket. As soon as I heard it, I saw it as a poster. It made itself, really," he admits. "Whatever medium I'm working in, the basic function is the same—to engage and amuse other people," he states.

Burrill's approach to image-making has won him many admirers, and he is in constant demand. It is his work for award-winning Dutch advertising agency KesselsKramer that he regards most highly, however. "The first time I worked for them was for the Hans Brinker budget hotel. That was my first 'big break.' Subsequently, I've worked on a couple of campaigns for Diesel with them," he recalls. "It's always great because they give me so much freedom. The results are always very pure and stand out from everything else."

Combining Processes

Working for print and screen both appeal to Burrill. Recent projects include creating Web sites for two of his favorite bands, Kraftwerk and Air. However, it is his love for a range of working methods that motivates and informs his work. "I'm interested in combining processes—drawings scanned in, then colored on the computer—or finding old techniques—photocopying and letterpress printing are still my favorites," he adds. "I always have a digital camera with me to record things, funny bits of type, or interesting buildings. I use the photos as starting points for drawings." He has yet to find a button on his camera that records a "smell," though.

3. Sock Kid, Sony PlayStation, character development
4. Work Hard & Be Nice to People, personal project, poster
5. London Underground, public service poster
6. *Magic Land*, personal project, limited-edition book

FOREST WITH CLOUD

1

Staring at album sleeves and painting motorcycle jackets was the inspiration for Brett Ryder.

Brett Ryder admits that getting a computer was a career-defining moment after his graduation from the Illustration Master of Arts program at Central St Martins College in London in 1994. His eclectic approach to image-making—he uses a combination of found images and ephemera collaged together with his own drawings—made the transition to digital an interesting one. Ryder has a fervent interest in old motorcycles, and rebuilds the manifold on his BSA 650 with a dexterity that translates well to his use of Photoshop to "build" his images.

"I did loads of stuff as a kid," offers Ryder about his route into image-making and illustration. "I was the one everyone came to when they wanted their favorite album or band painted on their leather jacket. I even had my own airbrush. We did have some strange characters turning up on our doorstep, though." Linked to that early career move, Ryder talks a little about his dream project. "I've always dreamed of doing the Rolling Stones tour stuff, stage props, animations for their videos, T-shirts, the whole deal."

2

1. *The Observer* newspaper, Satisfaction
2. *The Observer* newspaper, Hot Weather

Rock 'n' Roll

Music has always featured highly in Ryder's life. "Staring at album sleeves was once a full-time occupation," he admits, insisting that the once-stylish Roxy Music are his all-time favorite band. But he claims that finding "socks with no holes or, if lucky, a pair" is the right start to a creative day. Working from a studio at home, Ryder's sartorial elegance is no match for that of his hero Bryan Ferry. "I can sit around all day in my pyjamas, and nobody is any the wiser," he explains, in a manner that could best be described as tongue-in-cheek.

"It is all I Know"

Ryder's work is cheeky. It retains a playful quirkiness, first developed in his early student pieces, and combines the real with the unreal, the literal with the imaginary. Ryder's illustrations regularly greet readers of the UK's daily broadsheets—*The Guardian*, *The Independent*, and *The Times*—as well as *The Observer* on Sundays. It is, perhaps, the surreal nature of Ryder's images that works so well with the journalism published by the cream of the UK's newspaper industry.

Despite the constant flow of work, which includes projects for BP, NatWest Bank, and Penguin Books, Ryder worries about his fate. "The best thing about working as an illustrator is that it is all I've wanted to do and it is all I know," he states. "The worst thing about being in illustration is knowing it is all I know."

3. *The Guardian* newspaper, BMP advertising campaign
4. *The Observer* newspaper, Viagra
5. Heart Agency calendar

6. Kino Design, untitled
7. NB: Studio, Marchant
8. Economist Books, Negotiations

1

© S. KUBO/2004

Collaborations and exhibitions keep Seijiro Kubo inspired to "push" his client's interpretation of his work.

Seijiro Kubo made the transition from fully fledged graphic designer to illustrator/image-maker after a friend's chance remark. Upon graduation from the Nippon Designer's School, Kubo worked for a couple of years as a designer for a local graphic design company. By his own admission, he wasn't very good at it, and he decided to quit. "One day, a friend praised some illustrations that I had drawn for work," he states, matter-of-factly, "and that's when I chose to start my career as an illustrator."

Two Solutions

This choice has paid off. Kubo now works for numerous clients and exhibits his own self-initiated work on a regular basis, too. He is confident working in numerous

2

© S. KUBO/2004

1. Flower and Boy, personal project
2. Boy and Friend, personal project

Enjoy 100%. aiwa

We only have now.
So now is the time to play, laugh, enjoy.
Give it 100%.

3

4 # Enjoy 100%.

We only have now.
So now is the time to play, laugh, enjoy.
Give it 100%.

ways, so he approaches each project by creating two versions. "When I am offered a job, I go to meetings with the client to get a clear idea of the work they have in mind," he explains, "then I turn in two drawings. One is the one the client requested, and the other is the one I really want to push. After that, it's up to the client." It is a working method that works, as clients invariably opt for the more extreme versions that Kubo presents. "Basically," he adds, "all my rough drawing is done in an analog style," by which he means working with pencil or pen on paper. "I then do all of the brush-up work on the Macintosh."

Kubo feels most motivated by his work involving the development of characters. He collaborated with Tokyo agency butterfly•stroke for Copet, a Web-based animal adventure playground. This remains a genuinely enjoyable project for him, which he continues to update. Kubo understands the necessity for self-initiated projects such as Copet. The work led directly to a commission for a series of posters for Aiwa, the hi-fi specialists, and brought his work in this medium to new audiences.

The Importance of Freedom

As part of Kubo's drive to push his work into new areas, he constantly exhibits in Tokyo. This gives him the freedom to create new projects involving new ways of working. "For the exhibitions, I tend to draw in a completely new style," he says.

It is clear that Kubo's two areas of work—the professional commissions and the gallery exhibitions—continue to feed each other, but he does recognize a shortfall. "I think I'm a little impatient," he offers, as if waiting for the Mac's digital paint to dry was taking a little too long…

3. Lion, Aiwa, advertising campaign poster
4. Panda, Aiwa, advertising campaign poster
5. Laforet Grand Bazar 01, advertising campaign poster
6. Laforet Grand Bazar 02, advertising campaign poster
7. Bird, Aiwa, advertising campaign poster
8. Ape, Aiwa, advertising campaign poster

Tutorial 3:
Paul Burgess

Breathing new life into old images is an art-form from which Paul Burgess has built a fruitful career. Here he works with lost and found elements to advertise an international fashion retail company.

Paul Burgess has a unique fascination with junk shop, flea market, and secondhand bookstore finds. As indeed he might, with an appetite for creating one-off pieces of artwork that capture a bygone era with a timeless quality, he is the master of the collaged image.

Commissioned by Burro, a fashion label based in Covent Garden in London, Burgess was invited to create an image to run across a double-page spread in US magazine *Sport and Street*. In all, four different artists and designers were invited to create images for the campaign, which ran throughout a summer season. The brief was deceptively simple; Burgess was asked to create an image that conveyed his own interpretation of subjects that included youth culture, the UK, and Pop. Here is how he did that …

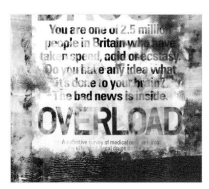

1 A found spread from a magazine is pasted onto board to create the base of the image. Burgess then handpaints roughly over areas to obliterate elements, leaving some of the image slightly revealed.

2 A second base area is created using paper that has been painted with gouache. At this point elements are created ready to use, but nothing is added until final design decisions are made.

3 Further base panels are made. This one is from an oddly shaped piece of black card. An important element in Burgess' collages is his lucky finds and how he then plans a usage for these pieces within his work.

7 As some of the base images are decided upon, they are placed in the final image. Some collage artists like to scan all of their chosen elements into the computer, then resize and reposition each element in Photoshop. For this project, Burgess works by hand.

4 A cardboard template used to make pom-poms is given a new life as an element in this piece of work. Often Burgess will have images for months before the right project to use them in crops up.

5 The famous Lucky Strike cigarette pack, this one found on the streets of Athens in Greece, is kept in a sketchbook for later use.

6 Scanned, resized, and printed onto acetate, the image forms part of the red circle behind the girl's head. No longer recognizable as a Lucky Strike pack, the image is used purely for its color and shape.

7 As some of the base images are decided upon, they are placed in the final image. Some collage artists like to scan all of their chosen elements into the computer, then resize and reposition each element in Photoshop. For this project, Burgess works by hand.

8 A found drawing, simply titled "Weird Kid," is cut out and detail is added, again by hand. Burgess works with each element lightly tacked in place before putting them together more permanently prior to scanning the final artwork.

9 The background shapes are now formatted and positioned. Burgess understands exactly how the composition may be structured at this stage, having worked out areas of the collage by placing and moving elements around until he is happy with the overall effect.

10 From a magazine found in a flea market in Barcelona, Spain, Burgess scans a drawing of a girl, and makes alterations in Photoshop, changing colors and resizing the image before printing out and trimming to size.

11 Here a section from an old football is removed, partly because of its interesting shape, but also because it has the word "rock" printed on it. It is these kinds of interesting finds that spark creative ideas in the collage artist's mind.

12 Another intriguing element with an interesting history is added to the images being used. An image taken from a long out-of-print children's book about making gifts is scanned, cleaned up, printed out, and utilized.

13 Other found elements are incorporated. Motifs of hearts, stars, and globes come together and are "printed" from photocopies using chemical paint thinners to transfer the image: a blurring effect is created using this method.

14 Weird Kid is cut away from any background material, and a touch of redrawing is done to strengthen some of the line work.

15 A similar process occurs with the printout of the girl from Barcelona. Additional handrendered details are added at this stage.

16 Rubber stamps have a unique feel when used in collaged images. Burgess adds a simple graphic to the found bunny before placing the image into the collage.

17 A lettering stencil found in a street market in New York is employed to add some typographic elements by hand. The text is inspired by lyrics from a song by The Libertines.

18 Once elements have slowly built up, the final image starts to take shape and all that remains is for Burgess to either photograph or scan the artwork so that the image file can be sent via e-mail. The image can also be stored as a digital file and Burgess is now free to reuse any of the elements in new work.

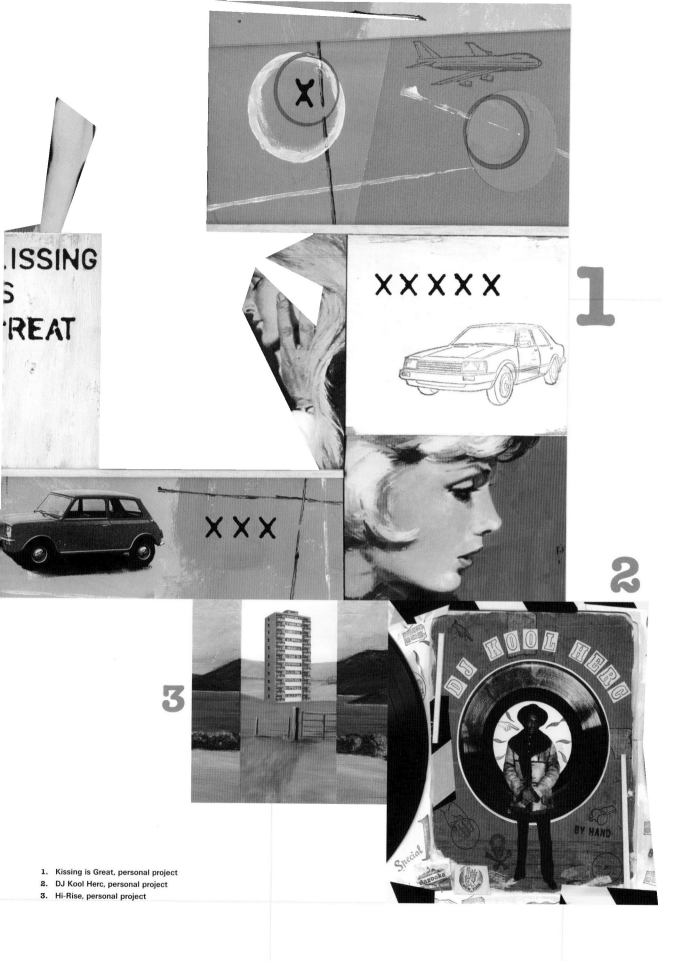

1. Kissing is Great, personal project
2. DJ Kool Herc, personal project
3. Hi-Rise, personal project

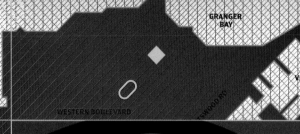

GRANGER
BAY

THREE ANCHOR BAY

WESTERN BOULEVARD

ROCKLANDS BAY

PELUQUERIA

YOU
REAP
WHAT
YOU SOW

SORTIDA

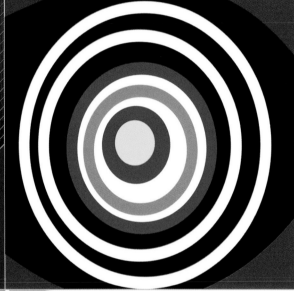

4

CA.

PALM
SPRINGS

AZ.

PHOENIX

TUCSON

NM

THIS PUB HAD
BETTER BE
WORTH IT

The Power of the Drawn Mark

"Everyone is an artist," claimed Germany's most recognized conceptual artist, Josef Beuys, although it is unclear if his statement extended through to the discipline of drawing.

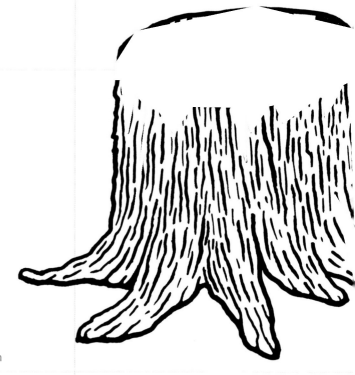

"Drawing is the honesty of the art. There is no possibility of cheating. It is either good or bad," said Spanish surrealist Salvador Dali. Dali died in 1989, but had he lived into the nineties and witnessed the birth of the digital revolution in design and image-making, he may have found his claim being severely tested. Software applications, emulating the techniques of painting and drawing, became increasingly sophisticated, and for a while it seemed that with the correct kit, the most up-to-the-minute application, and a how-to-do-it book beside the keyboard and drawing tablet, anyone with a modicum of talent could work as a digital artist.

Be an Artist—Be Your own Boss!

Training manuals, proclaiming to teach easy step-by-step lessons in drawing, were not new. In the US during the fifties, with consumerism, mass manufacturing, and mass marketing in abundance, a boom in graphic arts was evident, and advertisements for home-study courses featured in numerous publications. Reproductions of early ads found in *Mostly Happy Clip Art of the Thirties, Forties and Fifties* (Jerry Jankowski, 1992, the Art Direction Book Company, USA) features some prime examples. "stART drawing big money," one proclaims. "Be an artist and be your own boss," another promises, in a drive to attract customers to take up their offer of "commercial art, cartooning, and design—all in ONE practical course. "An ability to draw seemed not to be high on the list of priorities. "Create thousands of your own designs—no lessons, no talent—the first day," was the improbable claim put forward by another advertisement of the time.

1.   Jody Barton, Greenpeace, The Last Tree Gone
2.   Matthew Green, Sleaze Nation, Nintendo
3.   Brian Cairns, Howies, wardrobes
4.   Graham Carter, *Televisual* magazine, feature
5.   Jason Ford, personal project, Christmas card

6

7

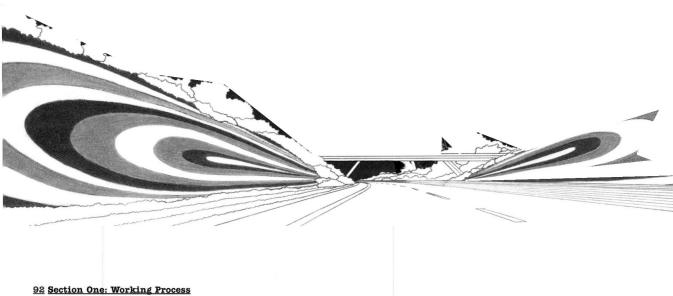

In H. A. Box and T. R. Dipple's book, *How to Draw and Paint Successfully*, also published in the fifties, clear distinctions were made between drawing for pleasure and drawing for profit. "The commercial artist is not selling art but using it to sell something else—a product or service, or even an idea. It is this product, service, or idea that matters most," the book explains. Suggesting that the commercial artist should neither get too precious about the process of drawing nor allow an "artist's ego" to hinder "the principles which govern his work," the book stands as a harsh reality check for those who believed in artistic growth or self-fulfillment through the medium. Despite this, the writers do offer some encouragement to the reader. "A career in commercial art can be interesting, satisfying, and financially rewarding," they state, in a very matter-of-fact manner.

6. Kam Tang, *Dazed & Confused* magazine, PORN?
7. Keiji Ito, VenusFort, advertising campaign
8. Elliott Thoburn, Sleaze Nation, Shoplifting

Art or Illustration?

The debate surrounding commercial artists, later to be viewed as either graphic designers or illustrators, was not a new phenomenon, even in the fifties. Arguments surround 30,000-year-old cave-paintings in Lascaux and Altamira: are they art or illustration? Both sites appear to have been focal points for religious and hunting rites so could be considered to have a functional purpose, highlighting the role of illustration over fine art, perhaps. Even if ancient Chinese picture-writing, Egyptian hieroglyphics, and hand-painted illuminated manuscripts are discounted as the starting point for the printed reproduction of the illustrated image, there is evidence of commercial art as early as the fifteenth century. Printed in 1472, Robertus Valturius produced woodcuts of military and naval equipment in a handbook for military leaders of the Renaissance, and it is known that Leonardo da Vinci owned a copy while he was working as chief engineer to Cesare Borgia. Illustration, unlike painting, did not receive favored recognition. Most Renaissance scholars and humanists regarded it as suitable only for the "vulgar and illiterate," illiteracy being the norm.

Drawn to Drawings

Drawing's link with fine art is inextricable, from Henri Matisse's observation that "drawing is like making an expressive gesture with the advantage of permanence," through to Andy Warhol's opposing description of the activity, as recorded in *The Andy Warhol Diaries*, published in New York in 1989. "I had a picture and I used the tracing machine that projects the image onto the wall and I put the paper where the image is and I trace." Warhol, although later recognized as one of the world's most important modern artists, had originally trained at Carnegie Institute of Technology, where he studied pictorial design. On arriving in New York from Pittsburgh, upon graduation in the summer of 1949, Warhol set to work as a commercial artist and illustrator, with much success.

8

9. Mr. Bingo, *Marmalade* magazine, subscription promotion
10. Paul Wearing, 340 Interiors, marketing for Chicago luxury development
11. Phil Hankinson, *Lucky* magazine, south-western cities shopping feature

In *Andy Warhol: Drawings 1942–1987*, Mark Francis and Dieter Koepplin make the assertion, based on the recollections of artist Philip Pearlstein, who graduated with Warhol and moved to New York at the same time, that his success was based on two significant factors. The first was Warhol's "simplicity of style," his work having acquired "its recognizably linear outline and signature economy." The latter was Warhol's "utter willingness to respond to demands from clients." It seems more evidence of the need that commercial artists would have to be willing to sell their own souls to achieve success.

Drawing as a Way of Thinking

Another modern artist, now employing within his work the stark digital graphic techniques most often used in design and illustration disciplines, is Julian Opie. His early drawings and sketches led to the development of his sculptures of household objects, constructed from painted steel. He recorded his own involvement with the discipline of drawing in a catalog accompanying an exhibition of his work at the Institute of Contemporary Art in London in 1985. The publication, a small, pocketbook-sized edition, features an introduction with an insight into Opie's approach. "These drawings are not an attempt to make a pleasing image, or to be finished works in themselves, but rather a way of thinking on paper in a language as immediate as writing," he states. Opie offers a very different take from Warhol on the process of drawing, but his is a valid description of his approach to the process.

12. Shonagh Rae, *Highlife* magazine, Vulture
13. Tom Barwick, Fuck Shit UP Skateboards, Survivalist
14. Tom Gauld, Capsule exhibition, Beer mat

15

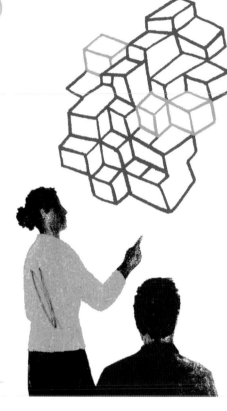

Unlocking the Creative Process

Drawing is a very personal, unique form of practice, whether conducted by the fine artist or the commercial artist. It can come naturally, and it can be improved upon by practice. The impact of real drawing ability, it can be argued, is evidenced in all manner of working methods as employed by today's graphic image-makers. Marshall Arisman, US illustrator and educator for over 40 years, explains in his book *The Education of the Illustrator*, a jointly edited venture with author and art director Steven Heller, that "drawing is an activity that demands practice to realize its full potential." Arisman goes on to state that "a good teacher can help, but drawing is not an end in itself. The process of drawing can unlock the entire creative process for an artist." These are wise words indeed, and a welcome respite from the advertisement claims from a bygone era.

Drawing and the Digital

The relationship that drawing has with the digital remains a sticky subject for some. Arisman explores the issue, stating that he is "fearful that most illustrators' choices about the computer are based on speed, greed, short cuts, and avoiding the practice itself." He suggests that each new drawing contains "memory of our past drawings until we die," adding that it is this memory that separates the activity of drawing from creating an image on the computer. "The tool has no personal memory that is not programmed in," he argues, sidestepping or ignoring the work of those who choose to combine the analog and the digital within their working methods.

It is the work of today's graphic image-makers—those using the mouse to draw, scanning pencil sketches into the computer, combining digital and handmade marks—that is pushing the discipline forward. Whether influenced by the diagrammatic and graphic look of instruction manuals, popular in recent years; simple, pixelated work, reminiscent of early PC screens; or the childlike innocence of "outsider art," it is clear that the drawn image remains as crucial and as inspirational today as it has been for previous generations.

16

I love you

1

The Vector Master who takes one job at a time, perhaps two...

For the guy who won a Creative Futures Award for best up-and-coming illustrator in 1998, Kam Tang's first commission was hardly the biggest job on the planet. The brief was for an image that measured 6 x 3cm (2⅜ x 1⅛ in) for a radio listing in the UK's *Radio Times* magazine. In the years since the award, though, Kam Tang has worked for clients in London, Tokyo, New York, Munich, and Amsterdam. Initially, recognized for the finest vector drawing abilities in town, Tang was commissioned by design group Graphic Thought Facility to create illustrations for the annual prospectus of The Royal College of Art (RCA), in London. Tang had studied at the RCA himself and knew how best to represent the hallowed sanctity of the place. He created a vast hand-drawn illustration of the exterior of the building using just a few minimalist vector lines. The real beauty of the piece was in its extremely detailed, full-colored rendering of the ice-cream truck that parked outside the RCA every day. The emphasis of the piece was so wrong yet so right.

2

3

Ideas First

Reflecting on his own design approach and philosophy, represented in the early RCA commission, Tang keeps it simple. "Ideas first." This simple approach, coupled with his unmatched vector drawing skills, has impressed a whole range of clients. Tang now counts CD sleeves for Merz, billboard and magazine advertising campaigns for Adidas, and identity work for The Design Museum in London among his favorite commissions.

Work has continued to flood in, and although Tang describes his role simply as "being my own boss and making my own works," it is clear that the flood is not without a certain level of pressure. Juggling deadlines, clients, and commissions from his studio at home in South London, Tang admits, "you can output an incredible amount of work in the final moments of an impending deadline, but never at the start!" Tang goes on to offer advice to aspiring illustrators, based on his own early experiences. "Never take on more than two jobs at once."

Watching Stanley Kubrick's movies, and old Bruce Lee kung-fu films, listening to Mozart piano sonatas, catching up on comic artworks created by Jack Kirby and George Herriman, and "investigating nature and science," as Tang puts it, are all key aspects of what influences him as an image-maker. New Yorkers Saul Steinberg, Milton Glaser, and Seymour Chwast are all admired by Tang too, but it is perhaps his own left-field take on the world that allowed him to see the beauty in that ice cream truck outside the country's highest seat of art and design learning.

Navigator
Cape Town

Wallpaper*
MARCH 2005
*INTERNATIONAL DESIGN INTERIORS LIFESTYLE

3. Two Culture Clash, *Two Culture Clash* CD sleeve artwork
4. *Wallpaper** magazine, Cape Town navigator map
5. *Wallpaper** magazine, cover illustration

New Resolution Number 1

GIVE UP SMOKING...

1

.... SOMEONE ELSES CIGARETTES.

2

An organized perfectionist, Spencer Wilson's approach and work ethic are, in his own words, "boring."

Spencer Wilson is boring—this is his own description. Reliable or efficient may be a more apt portrayal, although not according to Wilson. "My approach to work has always been quite boring. I always get jobs done on time. I make sure that I never work past 11.00pm, and, if I can, always anticipate what the client may ask for next," he says. "I make a regular point of visiting Zwemmers, Magma, and Waterstones bookstores in London so I can keep abreast of what is happening in design. The last book I bought was *Graphic Design for the 21st Century*. How boring is that?" asks Wilson. This singular vision and professional outlook, combined with a great eye, a sense of humor, and a unique way of working, has assisted Wilson in winning commissions as a busy image-maker.

The Lure of the Personal Project
As one-eleventh of illustration collective Peepshow, Wilson is another image-maker for whom the lure of the personal project and the exhibition is strong. Peepshow have held exhibitions for clients and friends at locations across East London, putting themselves on the map and, at the same time, creating traffic to their group Web site,

3

FEEL THE FLOW
PERVERTED EYE FUN

4

5

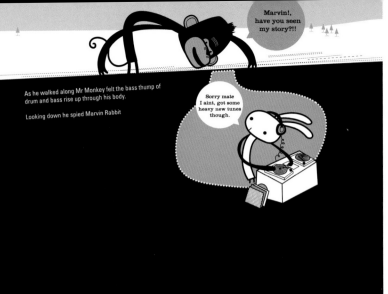

As he walked along Mr Monkey felt the bass thump of drum and bass rise up through his body.

Looking down he spied Marvin Rabbit

Marvin!, have you seen my story?!!

Sorry mate I aint, got some heavy new tunes though.

6 **7**

SCIENCE
LOVE

8

www.peepshow.org.uk. The members of Peepshow get together once a month to discuss projects and organize exhibitions and publications. These group events help to keep a sense of community in what can be a solitary existence. "The solitude is the toughest thing about working from a studio at home," explains Wilson. "I began working in a large basement living/work space in London, working with two other Peepshow members. The place was dark and rough around the edges, but the positive side was the landlord, a mad ex-photographer, who let us do what we liked," admits Wilson. "I worked on a small desk using a chair I found on the street and an orange iMac, which I loved."

Enjoy the Buzz

Wilson is organized at maintaining contacts. He advises, "see one industry person and get a further three contacts." He keeps in touch with his own clients through regularly e-mailing illustrated images that reflect his current interests and thoughts. A recent piece pictured three advertising creative types around a table responding to the question "How many Art Directors does it take to change a light bulb?" with the witty one-liner, "Does it have to be a light bulb?" It is this type of humor in Wilson's work, along with his neat, quirky, vector-drawn characters, that has led to him working on advertising campaigns for Ski, Buzz Airlines, and Sky Premier. "I enjoy the buzz of being briefed and creating drawings, and I like the lifestyle, working to my own agenda and getting personal projects out there too," explains Wilson, without even a hint of boredom.

6. *Monkey*, personal project, limited-edition book
7. *The Tale of Little Red Riding Hood*, personal project, limited-edition book
8. Science Love, e-mailed promotion

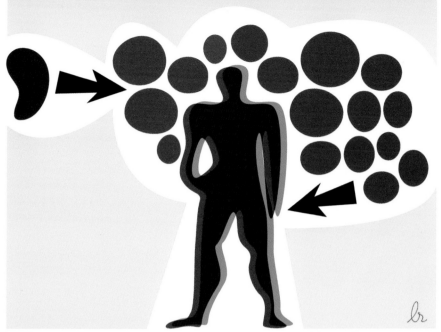

1

1. Diabetes, *The New Yorker*, article
2. I Want You, IKEA USA advertising campaign

2

"No job too large, no job too small, no job too medium-sized." Laurie Rosenwald takes on all comers.

Laurie Rosenwald is a New Yorker through and through, and proud of it. "I'm a native. I was born right here in Manhattan," she exclaims from her huge loft apartment just a couple of paces from the frenetic life of Canal Street. "I grew up in the city. My father was a sculptor, and I was always surrounded by art!" Rosenwald's studio continues the theme. In every direction you see more art: paintings, sculpture, prints, and collections of objects. "I remember wanting to be an artist from an early age, but not a fine artist. Being a fine artist is just trouble. I saw the financial problems my father had as an artist."

All Mushed Together
Rosenwald enrolled on an undergraduate course in graphic design at the Rhode Island School of Design (RISD) because she liked typography, "but it was all Swiss Univers and super-serious and I missed drawing.

3

snobbery
THE
AMERICAN
VERSION

JOSEPH
EPSTEIN

4

5

pepe Rosso

Laurie
Rosenwald

It was so humorless," she recalls. And humor plays a
large part in Rosenwald's work, together with her ability
to blur edges and resist the lure of the pigeonhole. "I then
went into illustration at RISD, but that didn't work. I went
back to graphic design but they wouldn't have me, so I
went on to painting. They just let me do what I wanted
to. Now what I do is painting, typography, and illustration
all mushed together."

Digital Love–Hate
Nowadays, Rosenwald divides her time between her loft
in Manhattan and Sweden, where she shares studio
space with a group of artists and designers, following an
artist-in-residence program she attended a few years ago.
Despite technology making life and travel easier—she
works on an Apple PowerBook that goes everywhere with
her—she has a love–hate relationship with computers.
"The computer brings people together in one way and
alienates them in another. I can create work in Sweden
for a client in Philadelphia but never meet them, or hear
their voice; it is all done by e-mail. I still find that strange."

New York—Soup to Nuts
Every project of Rosenwald's, although finalized and
transmitted digitally, starts with drawing. She draws by
hand using a dip pen and ink, often making up to 100
drawings. She likes to progress straight to the finished
product, so rarely creates visuals or roughs for clients.
"I don't do sketches; I just do it. It can be a pain though:
I sometimes feel I'm reinventing the wheel every time I
start a commission." Her approach has attracted a range
of clients that includes *The New Yorker*, Ikea, and Coca-
Cola, but it is her own book, *New York Notebook*, which
she wrote and designed, that has fired her imagination.
"People have always come to stay," she states. "I'm
always giving folk advice about what to see and do. It
made sense to put it in a book. New York—soup to nuts!"

Vector drawing is taken into fashion graphics as ilovedust, after working for numerous fashion-related companies, go it alone and create their own clothing range—a set of T-shirts.

ilovedust (ild) created their first clothing range. Having worked with some of the UK's finest high street names, they have a rare insight into fashion marketing. With this knowledge and a bunch of cool designs, ild launch their first range of T-shirts, sweats, and hoodies.

Bold graphic images, with more than just a whiff of street credibility and subtle humor, is an ild trademark. Working confidently with vector-driven software applications, ild have honed their digital drawing skills to perfection. Mastering the art of merchandising is not without difficulties, but ild understood their audience from the outset. "We didn't want to create a range with too much of a theme," explains Creative Director Mark Graham. "We just wanted to create quality garments with clever and individual branding."

1 For a simple-looking promotional T-shirt, the company logo—a freeform hand-rendered vector graphic previously created as part of the overall company identity—is imported into Illustrator. A dust cloud is drawn within the application using an original drawing on paper, scanned in for use as a template.

2 Both the logo and cloud icons, on separate layers, are duplicated and repeated. This is a simple action that would take hours of redrawing by hand.

3 The artwork for this T-shirt remains in black. The design is to be reproduced in various colorways, but always as a one-color print. Therefore, creating the artwork in a single, bold color gives the best results when transferred for screen printing.

4 A quirky design, inspired by tourists, sees a camera casually slung around the neck of the T-shirt. From a distance, the impression is of a real camera, but close-up it is clear that this is a well-executed graphic drawing. It starts life as a photograph of the chosen camera.

5 Using the photograph of the camera, scanned into the computer, the image is created as a vector drawing, then output so that handrendered detail can be added. This helps make the image look less diagrammatic and gives it a more personal, sketched feel.

6 Taken back into the computer, the rescanned image is cleaned up and finalized. Small areas are retouched in Photoshop to produce the artwork that will be used to make the screens for printing.

7 Vector-drawing skills are utilized, once again, for another branded T-shirt image. With old-school computer and console games as inspiration, a simple logo, with the visual effect of pixelation, is created.

8 In Illustrator, the vector icon is distorted using one of the application's effects. A simple operation that allows the logo to be transformed in moments, this effect is best used in small doses.

9 At this stage, the results of the effect are evident—a slight distortion gives the impression of perspective. The opening credits of the classic 1977 movie *Star Wars* is still an impressive visual reference for designers.

10 With the logo tilted slightly, a vector edge is created to give the impression of depth. This is a simple, yet effective technique and transforms a flat, 2-D image into one that looks more 3-D.

11 To create added interest, the original logo layer is repeated, resized, and slightly off-set, and has a different color applied.

12 Various color options are explored, both on screen and on printed samples. The positioning of the printed image on the shirt also has to be considered. In the studio, sample shirts and digital printouts are ironed into position.

13 ild work collectively on group projects. They draw advice and creative suggestions from each other. The studio provides a hothouse of talent, and projects such as this get the designers interacting constantly.

14 A photograph of the T-shirts demonstrates the numerous options in print and garment color. Variety ensures that the range has longevity and that each shirt feels more individual than other mass-produced versions available.

1. Insects, Lucky 3, wall panel

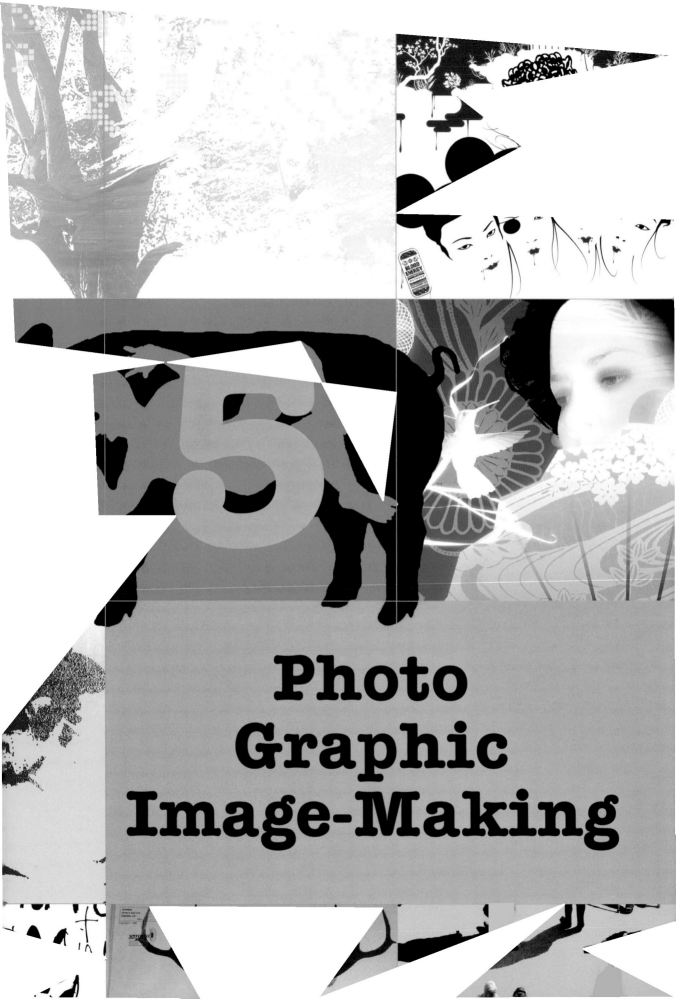

Photo
Graphic
Image-Making

1

With edges starting to blur and the boundaries between skills far less distinct, the graphic image-maker, in incorporating digital photographic images in his/her work, stands across the divide between two disciplines.

Contemporary image-makers know no boundaries. They employ a range of techniques, whenever appropriate, without fear of crossing borders or demarcations between disciplines. As confident with a mouse as a pencil, as savvy with a drawing tablet as a digital camera, they fearlessly adopt and adapt processes and methods of working with little regard for the historical baggage that accompanies some aspects of art, design, and photography. This freedom stems from being at the forefront of a discipline that does not follow a single medium of expression, thus allowing the image-maker opportunities for crossover and the merging of processes. Following migration from the analog to the digital, many image-makers turned their attention to formats that would capture real life and that could be returned to the studio ready and available for editing and modifying. The answer lay with the digital camera.

Believe in Photographs

At the dawn of traditional photography, the medium struggled to gain recognition as an independent art form; it was viewed to be in direct opposition to painting. Historically, reactions have been less than positive. Picasso proclaimed, "I have discovered photography. Now I can kill myself. I have nothing else to learn."

Years later, British photographer David Bailey hit back, "It takes a lot of imagination to be a good photographer. You need less imagination to be a painter, because you can invent things. But in photography everything is so ordinary; it takes a lot of looking before you learn to see the ordinary." Ansel Adams, US photographer and environmentalist, recorded his views, "Not everybody trusts paintings, but people believe photographs," he stated.

1. Neasden Control Centre, Agent Deck/Rome Snowboards, skate deck design
2. Shonagh Rae, personal project, Australia
3. Insect, personal project, POW Poster—01
4. Insect, personal project, POW Poster—02
5. Insect, personal project, POW Poster—03

2

3

4

5

In commercial design, advertising, and publishing, the photographer, it would appear, has always been held in greater regard than the illustrator, commanding higher fees, demanding expenses, and hiring and firing assistants. The mystique surrounding the professional photographer has been utilized to great effect. Mainly due to the perceived complexities of camera and darkroom equipment, this technology has served to reinforce preconceptions. As the PC and associated desktop publishing boom of the late eighties and nineties opened the medium to the home user, so too did the introduction of the digital camera. Digital advances, quite simply, changed the landscape of photography.

From Spy Satellites to Video Freeze-Frame
The digital camera has its origins in spy satellites, with government backing in digital technology, but the private sector also made major contributions. Texas Instruments were the first to patent a filmless electronic camera, in 1972, and nine years later, Sony released the Sony Mavica electronic still camera. The first commercial electronic camera, it recorded images onto a mini disc that had to be put into a video reader connected to a TV monitor or color printer. Despite kickstarting a revolution, the Sony Mavica can't truly be considered a digital camera; it was a video camera that took video freeze-frames.

Kodak, working to advance digital technology since the mid-seventies, had invented several solid-state image sensors that would convert light to digital pictures, but it wasn't until 1986 that Kodak scientists announced the world's first megapixel sensor. Capable of recording 1.4 million pixels, the sensor could produce a 7 x 5in digital, photo-quality print. In 1987, Kodak released seven new products for recording, storing, manipulating, transmitting, and printing electronic still video images. In 1990 they introduced the Photo CD system and with that, developed the first global standard for defining color in the digital environment. In 1991, Kodak launched the first truly digital camera system (DCS), aimed at professional photojournalists, in the shape of the Nikon F3 camera. This was fully equipped with a 1.3-megapixel sensor.

14

15

16

The "Serial Killer"

Consumers had to wait another four years for a camera that would work with a home computer. Apple, in another industry coup, launched the Apple QuickTake 100 camera in February 1994 at the MacWorld Expo in Tokyo, 10 years after the groundbreaking Macintosh had arrived. Shaped like a pair of binoculars and finished stylishly in matte gray, the QuickTake 100 introduced a new file format, QuickTake, that used QuickTime to decompress images. Dubbed the "serial killer" due to the camera's "plug and play" connectivity via a simple cable rather than the complicated SCSI connections found in all other peripheries of the time, the camera worked on both Mac and PC platforms. A review of the Apple QuickTake 100 in *Digital Imaging Plus* magazine, one month after Apple's launch of the camera, reads like the first reviews of the iMac and iPod years later, describing the camera as a "simple but well designed 'sexy' product that is fun and easy to use." The reviewer saw the future in the QuickTake 100. "If it catches on, it will be the forerunner of a line of products which could change the way that families take, manage, and print their social pictures," they predicted.

Despite Apple standing on the brink of a digital photography revolution, the QuickTake 100 would prove, as *Digital Imaging Plus* magazine had predicted, to be just the "forerunner" of advances in new digital camera technology. A year into Apple's lead in this key aspect of the digital domain, Kodak launched the DC40. This was followed by Casio's premier of their QV-11, the first digital camera with an LCD monitor, later the same year. Sony entered the market in 1996, with the Cyber-shot digital still camera. However, it was Kodak, aided by a huge marketing campaign, that put digital photography

in the public consciousness. In collaboration with Microsoft and Kinkos, Kodak created digital image-making software kiosks and workstations, enabling customers to create photo CD discs, enhance and manipulate photographs, and add digital images to documents. Soon after, Hewlett-Packard launched the first color printers designed to complement digital camera images. Where the Polaroid camera, invented by American physicist Edwin Land and first launched in 1948, had offered the public instant images, the digital camera went many steps further.

Radical Shifts

The digital camera is perhaps so remarkable because it has been such a radical shift from its predecessor. Dependent on chemical and mechanical processes, the conventional camera uses a series of lenses that focus light onto a piece of film to create an image. The digital camera, also through the use of lenses, focuses light onto an image sensor that records electronically; a computer then translates this information into digital data. With camera prices falling, specifications improving, and digital photographic images in a format easily imported into editing software, it has been no surprise that photography and graphic image-making have begun to merge so seamlessly in recent years.

As a reference tool, the digital camera has proven invaluable: easy-to-use, small, portable, and relatively inexpensive to purchase. For the image-maker who draws from visual reference materials, bringing instant images into the computer as a starting point is a straightforward process. Taking one's own images, rather than relying on printed reference material in books, means that there is no shadow of copyright infringement. Taking away the

reliance on images from stock reference libraries or trawling the Web gives back much of the creativity to the image-maker. Setting up, taking images, and importing them into the relevant software application to use as reference material has become second nature to many contemporary creative image-makers.

Blurring Edges

For those who choose to work more directly with the photographic image, incorporating it into their work or making it the main aspect of their creative process, rather than using it simply as a source of reference material, the digital camera has helped create entirely new working methods and results. The introduction of screen printing into fine art, in the early sixties, could be viewed as a forerunner to this approach. Artists in the US, among them Robert Rauschenberg, used the process of screen printing to bring a raw realism to picture-making through the use of the photographic in combination with paint and collage. Here was a technique that allowed the direct reproduction of a photographic image onto the surface of a painting or collage. The digital camera, combined with the computer and associated software applications, has given the image-maker the same powers within the digital domain.

As edges blur and the distinctions between boundaries become less well defined, questions are being asked about the role of the photographer and the illustrator. Where these areas of crossover merge, bleeding from one to another, is where today's image-makers stand.

SHOW YOU NATURAL UNIFORM

18

MUTADOR
WWW.MUTADOR.COM
Fotógrafo: Man
Modelo: Sergio
Diseño: info@mutador.com
UNDRESS CODE XX

19

Previous page
17. Joe Magee, Taunton and Somerset Hospital Trust, Occupational Therapy B

This page
18. Mutador, *Blank* magazine, Uniforms
19. Vault49, *DEdiCate* magazine, No. 06

1

2

Filmmaking, exhibiting illustrator finds creative freedom in saying "No!"

Joe Magee has lived in many cities in the UK. Having studied in his hometown of Liverpool before moving on to the London College of Printing and then, at MA level, Manchester Metropolitan University, Magee has finally made Bristol his home. His name is now inseparably linked, across the city, with an exhibition he held at Watershed Arts Centre, Bristol's cultural melting pot. People often say "ah yes, the rabbits," as they nod in recognition if you mention Magee's name. The rabbits were part of an animated piece about memetics and mind viruses which included endlessly replicating white rabbits on a red background. These have, according to Magee, "found their way into many people's psyches. So the idea seems to have worked."

Independent Thinking

Magee's images garner responses from his audience. He provokes reactions through his work, and finds he is commissioned because his work has a point of view. He cites his most memorable job as the Penguin cover for Anthony Burgess' novel *A Clockwork Orange*. His heroes include Peter Saville, Andy Warhol, Vincent Van Gogh, David Lynch, and William Heath Robinson, so it is clear that he has a high regard for other independent thinkers and creators.

Having utilized digital media for many years, Magee has developed a creative visual within his images that imbues them with an individuality, a unique look and feel.

1. Host, *Libération* magazine, feature
2. Heart of Chairs, *The Observer* newspaper, article

3

Magee puts this down to retaining creative freedom. "I've never been motivated by making lots of money, and I think this has really helped facilitate creative development. I've always felt compelled to remain independent and tried to feel comfortable about what jobs I'll accept. The reality of saying 'no' to big bucks for an artistically or ethically challenged job is harsh, but always feels good in the end," he explains.

Independent Projects

Magee works at a prolific rate. He has to, with two illustrations for national newspapers to create every week of the year, before he takes anything else on. Other Illustration commissions continue to arrive on a regular basis. "I've always had a steady stream of work from the US, having worked for *The New York Times*, *The Boston Globe*, and the *Los Angeles Times*. I've also worked regularly for *Libération* in France for many years."

It is extra-curricular projects that keep Magee motivated. Recently completed are three award-winning films about addictive behavior set on a deprived housing estate. "I'm becoming more and more interested in making films. I've found it difficult to stop making films. I've made about 10 in the last five years and am getting more commissioned," explains Magee. On top of the illustration and filmmaking, Magee exhibits. "I like the freedom in taking on independent, noncommercial projects, like generating a series of large digital prints for an exhibition at an interesting gallery," he says.

This is one independent, filmmaking, gallery-exhibiting illustrator who will continue to make the most of his creative freedom.

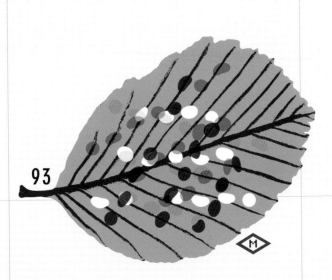

4

5

6

3. Clique, *The Observer* newspaper, article
4. Eden500, personal project, interactive digital artwork
5. Leaf Virus, *The Guardian* newspaper, article
6. Blackbird, personal project, digital artwork

Profile: McFaul

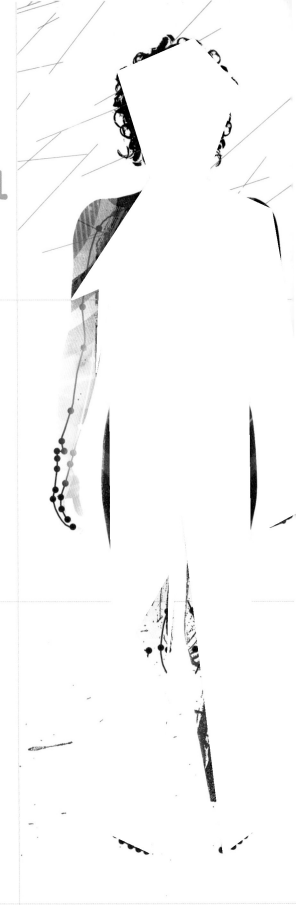

1

Mellow jazz, sixties' graphics, and the spirit of collaboration push the right buttons for McFaul, a man who time forgot.

"I've always been interested in and influenced by graphic image-makers; Saul Bass, Paul Rand, Woody Pirtle, and Kurt Schwitters. That whole generation of designers and artists who really kicked off in the sixties," explains McFaul from his newly converted loft/studio. Sitting in a chair that can best be described as a "we've been expecting you Mr. Bond" affair, with the mellow jazz sounds of Craig Armstrong playing in the background, McFaul could easily be mistaken for the man who time forgot. Until you see his work, that is.

Graphical Thinking

"I think quite graphically. I start with doodles that represent my thinking and move onto a list of ingredients," states McFaul, recounting a process that might equally describe the work of a jazz musician. "I collaborate with designers, rather than working for them," he muses. "I'm interested in the process over the esthetic," However, the esthetic remains crucial within his work—a beautiful synergy of the drawn and the photographic merged with pattern, with color, and with skill and dexterity that belies McFaul's origins in the print studio. "My work has been arrived at through the time I spent printmaking," he explains. "I enjoyed the experimentation and the things that went wrong; in fact, if it went wrong, it was so right."

1. I'm Thinking of Tron, *The Economist* magazine, feature
2. Winter, *Digital Creative Arts* magazine, cover image

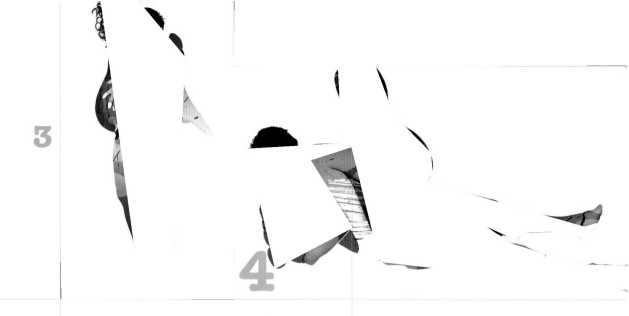

From Analog to Digital

The migration from analog to digital worlds was a relatively painless operation brought about by necessity. "I began getting too much work. I just thought, I can do color separations in minutes and hours on screen, rather than days in the print studio," McFaul admits. Having worked on a PC before moving to Apple, he now works across three machines in his studio, and uses a laptop when on the road.

Never without his camera, McFaul travels most places with it, his laptop, and an external drive in a bag. "I shoot stuff all of the time, every day," he explains. "I use figures in my work; they're generally friends, family—people I know mostly, although I do have to shoot some people without their knowledge," McFaul states, describing his use of the figure as if it were simply part of his list of chosen ingredients. A recent client, Publix, a supermarket chain based in Florida, commissioned McFaul to create a range of packaging for their sodas, and some tight restrictions forced a new approach. For the first time, working with a professional model, he was able to seek out someone of the exact profile described in the client brief.

Technology Enabled

It is where the edges between disciplines meet and blur that now interests McFaul. "I see more and more photographers digitally manipulating their images, and more and more illustrators using digital photography," he explains. "As image-makers, we can do anything that we want; the technology now allows it." McFaul celebrates the freedom open to today's graphic image-maker. "At art school, I could draw, so tutors actively pushed me toward illustration, but what I needed was the freedom to explore graphic design, fine art, illustration, and photography. And that's all I do now. The point is in doing something new every day." And right on cue, like the title of a hit by a sixties' jazz ensemble, he adds "It's what life is all about!"

3. Love, *Men's Health* magazine, Germany, feature
4. Love, *Men's Health* magazine, Germany, feature
5. *Mind Wide Open*, book jacket

1

2

It is a surreal journey that has led Josh Gosfield to the Mighty House of Pictures. "It's a pleasure to serve you."

It wasn't always this way for Josh Gosfield. As an untrained graphic designer—unless a year spent studying Agricultural Engineering at Cornell University in Ithaca, upstate New York counts—he arrived in New York City to work as a magazine art director. "I've always taught myself everything," Gosfield admits. "The bottom of the learning curve is where I like to be," he adds with a smile.

In 1994, after an eight-year stint as Art Director on *New York* magazine, Gosfield left commercial design to work as an image-maker. He has never regretted the move. "I was possessed of the naive misconception that the work would be done in some highly creative hothouse environment," Gosfield states. "I enjoyed the social aspect, the late-night deadline pressure, but I found the experience corporate, hierarchical, and often boring."

Life is anything but boring now. In a strangely corporate offices-to-rent building, a few blocks from the Holland Tunnel entrance in Manhattan, is Gosfield's studio—a manic and chaotic space where he busily employs a vast range of media. Surrounded by plaster-cast models, boxes of toys, theater props, and thrift-store cast-offs, along with vast numbers of aging magazines, books, and posters, Gosfield creates work with a passionate energy.

1. Saint of the Month: Castor/Pollux, personal project
2. Cat Girls, personal project

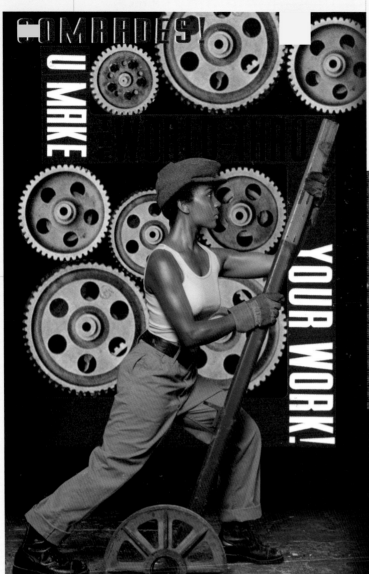

COMRADES!

U MAKE

YOUR WORK!

3

4

SANTO

CHINGON

5

From Fine Art to Commercial Art

Working across disciplines, stepping from fine art into commercial art and back again, whether making installations for the windows of Barney's, (New York City's coolest fashion department store, in Chelsea), or creating artworks for MTV, Nike, Levi's, or Sony, Gosfield happily breaks the mold. "I love everything. I love learning the new thing. I love combining various art forms," he exclaims. "Maybe it's self-sabotage, but as soon as I start getting comfortable with a craft, I get bored and want to move on." Gosfield admits to a demanding working process. "The thrill factor, for me, is higher when I really don't know what I'm doing."

A Brutal Ecstasy

6

Not knowing what he's doing includes shooting his subjects for inclusion in an image on a Nikon DX1 camera. "I'm mostly digital now. The digital world is changing so fast that it's a blast to be hooked up to all of that," he states, in a manner that belies his knowledge of the subject. With a Web site that welcomes the visitor to The Mighty House of Pictures, gallantly offering "It's a pleasure to serve you" as the corporate mantra, Gosfield is aware of his influences. The site, itself credits "all the great artists and hacks, Mexican sign painters, prison tattoo artists, and pornographers" who have inspired him. "Maybe it's a kind of brutal ecstasy I'm thrown into by great art, or moments in life," he suggests. "It could as easily be a guy loping down the street with a cocky gait and a hat cocked at an insane angle on his head as it can a painting."

Recent projects show Gosfield diversifying once again; he has written, produced, directed, edited, and scored a 20-minute, live-action film that is doing the rounds of the independent film festivals. He is still in search of the next dream project. "I have too many to list—theater sets, feature-length film, giant photos on lightboxes, huge altars in Times Square ..." All very far removed from magazine art direction or agricultural engineering.

Tutorial 5: McFaul

Increasingly, McFaul finds himself commissioned because of the blend of processes and techniques he employs.

Virgin Atlantic commissioned McFaul to work on a project that involved creating images to be used as stickers for VIP baggage, as a limited-edition, signed and numbered poster/print, and for use on a select range of T-shirts. With the design company involved in the project based in Miami, and McFaul based in the UK, communication and liaison was done via e-mail and the Web. McFaul describes the project as a "dream job." The client, a big fan of his approach, kept expanding the commission into new media as they became increasingly excited with his work.

McFaul uses a combination of techniques that derive from his initial use of the camera; he often shoots his own models and materials for a project. His working process then involves taking these digital images back to the studio for manipulating in Photoshop and Illustrator. The results speak for themselves.

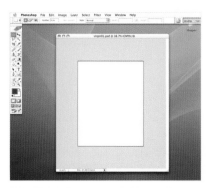

1 The blank canvas, or in this case the white of the screen, is always a daunting start for the image-maker. This is where it all begins.

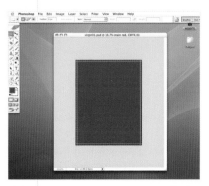

2 In Photoshop, the entire screen is filled with a color picked from the Virgin palette of chosen hues. The process of selecting and starting with a base color kicks the image off.

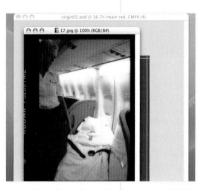

3 The client, Virgin Atlantic, have provided some visual material. This image of the interior of an aircraft is too small to be of any real use in the final image, but acts as a useful reference point.

4 While the supplied photograph can't be used within the artwork—the file resolution is too low—the image can be vector traced in Illustrator.

5 Further vector tracing starts to identify seats and windows within the image. Subtle use of line ensures that these background shapes give a sense of the location, but not in any great detail at this stage.

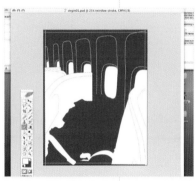

6 Further work starts to visually describe elements of the interior. This aspect of the process can be time-consuming, but attention to detail is vital.

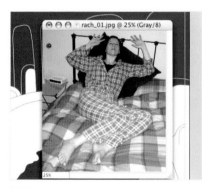

7 A photographic image, one of McFaul's own, is imported into the document. McFaul shoots real people as visual reference. This image is to be a startlet waking from a restful slumber on board a Virgin flight from London to Los Angeles.

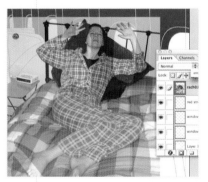

8 The photographic reference is traced using vector lines as shown previously. Once an image is in the computer, it can become integral to the working process.

9 With superfluous details removed, the photographic image is imported into the original artwork file. The girl now appears to be waking in the Virgin interior.

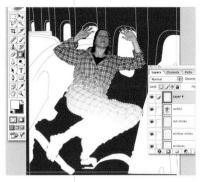

10 The nature of the brief demands that the final image is maximalist and decadent in look and feel. Here McFaul creates a linear gradient in white. He treats gradients, blurs, and layer blending with sensitivity: too much and the image can look overworked.

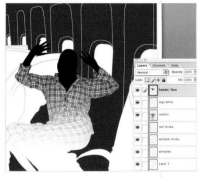

11 The composition is adjusted. Flipping the figure fits the piece better. It is always a good idea to spend time making images from various sources look convincing.

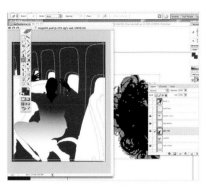

12 At this point McFaul adds elements of vector art from what he calls his armory—a folder on his computer. Having images to hand can save valuable time that would otherwise have to be spent redrawing.

13 A number of Illustrator vector files are combined to create the hair on the model, contributing to the sense of the "starlet."

14 A face is imported into the image to give some kind of reality to the figure. This is done quite roughly at this stage—improvements will be made later.

15 Further manipulation takes place, improving the image through blending modes and working with channels. This is the best route in getting under the skin of an application.

16 The image has to have a really strong graphic quality, so it makes sense to adjust the look of the pyjamas. By removing the check from the pyjamas and replacing it with vertical stripes, the shape of the body will be better defined.

17 Removing the horizontal lines is time-consuming, but an hour spent working in Photoshop will resolve the pyjamas visually. They are a vital aspect of the image and so demand this level of attention.

18 The effect of the pinstripes is to flatter the woman's figure and to suggest cosiness—exactly the values that Virgin are looking to communicate.

19 Stars and ribbons are added from the "armory" to give a more magical feel to the image. Importing vector images from Illustrator into Photoshop is a simple procedure and makes best use of the differences in the applications.

20 An additional ingredient is brought into the image; this time snow adds to the overall effect, imported as Illustrator files once again.

21 The composition is checked and rechecked, and the figure moved slightly to the right. These subtle shifts can make all the difference.

22 Some further work on the face, sensitively playing with the blending modes and channels on several layers, creates a look more in keeping with the feel of the image.

23 One aspect of the brief detailed the importance of including the flight number, 24, and the Virgin logo on the pyjamas. These are considered during the design stages, but only added toward the end of the process.

24 The logo is imported, with some skewing and retouching undertaken to create an element that sits well visually within the context of the image. This is a time-consuming process; blending photographic reference with digital drawing can take time.

1.   Love, *Men's Health* magazine, Germany, feature

Section Two: Professional Practice

Professional Practice

TIPS AND ADVICE FOR TODAY'S IMAGE-MAKERS

Want to be a professional image-maker? Or you already are, but fancy picking up on some tips that may just have passed you by? Well, here they are. In bite-sized nuggets, the tips and tricks that could put you ahead of the field!

1. A Killer Portfolio

What makes that killer portfolio? Why will one type of presentation always win over another? How can the way you present your work affect the fees clients are prepared to pay for it? Should you show every piece of work that you have ever produced? Which format of portfolio will work best for your needs? Do image-makers still need old-fashioned binders or will a CD or online presence deliver the goods?

This first section investigates the dos and don'ts of your portfolio presentation. We look at how to present your work to its best advantage and which format is best for you and your potential clients. Important advice about selecting and pacing the work you show, as well as tips on what to spend your money on, is given below.

1. Depending on who you plan to work for, you are still likely to need that old-fashioned leather portfolio with plastic sleeves. Clients like something printed in front of them. It works in meetings and does not suffer from compatibility problems! Buy the best that you can afford.

2. Spend wisely. Buy a leather portfolio. It will save you money in the long run. Leather will wear much better than plastic. It says that you take pride in your work and may even help you command higher fees!

3. You live and die by the quality of your portfolio. Your work may be up against work by other image-makers. Win the job. Make sure that your portfolio is well presented. Clean or change the plastic sleeves in your folder on a regular basis. Good presentation is a must!

4. Be clear about what your portfolio says. You may not be with your work every time it is viewed, so it must speak for itself. Keep it clear, concise, and precise. Present a positive image. Choose your strongest work—work that you feel positive about. Don't include anything you may have to apologise for!

5. Who is your portfolio for? You need it to show potential clients what you can do. Your clients, usually designers or art directors, may need to show it to their clients to get approval. Your portfolio must be able to speak to a whole range of different audiences. Remember this when you put it together.

6. Other tips for professional portfolios. Get into the habit of regularly adding new printed work as you produce it, keeping your folio fresh and up-to-date. Make sure that the running order makes sense—group work together depending on the type of client it was produced for.

7. Kick off your portfolio with your strongest image and end on an equally high note. These are the most important images in your book. Keep a list of exactly what is in your portfolio and the order it was in—clients will rearrange it!

8. Create at least two, maybe three portfolios, if you are planning on being busy. Many designers and art directors simply don't have time to meet all image-makers and want you to "drop off." Having more than one portfolio to circulate means no dead time.

9. With more than one portfolio, you never run the risk of being called in for that lucrative advertising commission at very short notice and not having a folio to hand. This happens. Be prepared and keep one portfolio sitting next to the phone.

10. Web sites. Important, useful, and a great complement to that leather-bound folio. A Web site will greatly add to your client base. Directing clients to your site means that they can view your work whenever, wherever. Cut your courier bill by not having to ship your portfolio all over town and across the globe!

11. Be creative with your site. Use it to showcase commissioned work, noncommissioned work, and even work in progress. Remember to update your site on a regular basis and let people know that you have done so.

12. The interactive CD-ROM should not be overlooked. Being able to leave this portfolio with clients is cool, so long as it works with their kit and is bug free! Think about your audience, Will they appreciate your extra costs in time, energy, and materials?

13. Think carefully about the work you show. Clients won't want to see a couple of drawings from an evening class you did over 10 years ago! Make sure that the work all sits together well and does not cover too many "styles." Be excellent at one way of working, not average at lots!

---

2. The Art of Self-Promotion

You are doing some great work. You know that you are. Your portfolio is looking great. You think you have this caper all worked out—just sit tight and wait for the phone to ring. Alas, nobody yet knows who you are and what you do, nor how to contact you. So how do you attract clients? How do you lead them to your online presence and presents? Get yourself some promotional items and quick!

Should your promo take the form of printed matter or does it matter if you e-mail your intended audience a selection of low-res images? For image-makers, the art of self-promotion is never over. Start as you mean to go on by following this set of guiding lights.

1. The original format for image-makers promoting their work is the postcard. Full-color image on one side and one color on reverse for contact details. Cheap, cheerful, and quick to produce. They fit in the sleeve inside your portfolio too. Beat that!

2. The unit cost of a postcard goes down the more you have printed. Before you order 1,000, though, think about whether you will use them all before you are sick and tired of the image. Look at the costs of shorter runs using a digital press rather than off-set litho.

3. You could get together with other image-makers and take a whole sheet; postcards are printed either 16 or 32 up. It will work out cheaper, but could be a hassle. If it doesn't suit, play the card printers off against each other to get the best price.

4. Postcards make sense but may seem boring. Think about other formats that you could adopt. Calendars have a one-year shelf life, if they are liked and used. Desk tidies are passé and should not be considered!

5. Your final choice of self-promo should show an image, your name, and contact details such as Web address, e-mail address, and phone number. This sounds straightforward, but many image-makers concentrate on the image and forget the details.

6. Get your work in annuals. Art buyers in advertising agencies swear by them. The pay-per-page image-making annuals like *Contact*, published by Contact, and *The Art Book*, publsihed by John Pigeon Publishing, are not cheap at between £600 and £1,000 (US $1,168 and $1,950) per page, but many image-makers claim they work better than anything else.

7. Send out a press release to all design magazines and journals when you create high-profile work. Send good, large-format transparencies as well as a concise "story" about the job. The design press have pages to fill and you can provide the content. Hey presto—free publicity!

8. Enter your work into national and international competitions. Many of the big organizations produce thick, glossy annuals of the best work. Some run touring exhibitions as well, along with Web sites that feature the work. Check the design press for details.

9. From your Web site, sell limited-edition, signed digital prints. Not all publicity material has to be given away. Encourage users to download free screen savers that you have created. Imagine your work on the screen of a computer in a busy design studio.

10. Don't spam! Nobody wants mail that they did not ask for. Once you have started to work for a client, they may be happy to receive a regular e-mail newsletter or set of low-res images, but wait until they are clients.

11. Contact galleries. Hold an exhibition of your work and invite clients and potential clients to a private view. Once again, let the design and local press know well in advance. On the night, stay off the wine and use the event to make contacts and meet new faces.

12. Don't waste money on getting mouse mats made up with your work on. Most designers (not all) use Macs, and the Apple Pro Mouse killed off the mouse mat!

13. Keep clients, and prospective clients up-to-date with what you are doing. Spend time and cash to create new publicity, showing how your work is evolving. Have a long-term plan for maintaining contact with your clients and creating new ones.

3. Identifying Clients, Making Contacts (and keeping them)

You have a portfolio itching to be seen and some publicity to die for. What you need now are some clients—or at least some potential ones! There is little point in showing work that features fantasy sci-fi space scenes to a design company specializing in annual reports for city clients! Get wise. Don't waste your time or that of others; target your work precisely. Be clear about what you do and who you wish to work for. Follow these tips to get right on track.

1. Think about buying lists of "creatives" from companies that specialize in this area. For a reasonable fee you could have the name of all the art buyers and creative directors in the top 200 advertising agencies. Think about how much time on the phone that could save you.

2. Spend time conducting some research. If you want to create images for magazines, browse through them over coffee in places like Borders. Target the right folks; try art editors and art directors rather than editors and writers.

3. Every time you see an interesting book jacket or CD sleeve, make it your mission to discover who created it and who commissioned it. Send the commissioning designer a copy of your publicity if you think that your work fits. Follow it up with a phone call to make an appointment to show your portfolio.

4. Be polite on the telephone and keep a pen to hand to write notes. Make sure that you have sent samples/publicity in advance. Trying to explain what your work looks like over the telephone is not easy!

5. Invest in a good database application and get used to updating it with new information on a regular basis. Enter a broad range of fields that includes the obvious—names, addresses, and contact details—as well as the type of company and the last time that you mailed publicity or made contact.

6. Whenever you visit a potential client, arrive a few minutes early. This gives you time to sit in the reception area and browse through their recent publicity, or current publications. A little knowledge can go a long way.

7. Be patient. Explain your work carefully, but do not outstay your welcome. Most designers, art buyers, and art directors will be able to give you just 10–15 minutes. Make this time count; keep focused on the work you want them to see, and be ready to exit!

8. Take a notebook to every meeting with a client. Take notes if you need to, and if they like your work ask them to recommend art directors and commissioners that you could visit at other companies. Word of mouth can be a real benefit.

9. Be prepared to "drop off" your portfolio rather than always meet person to person. If you would like a client to leave comments, provide a piece of paper taped to the inside of your portfolio, and remember to put fresh promo cards in too.

10. Keeping clients is a huge part of the job. If you are a pleasure to deal with, you are likely to get repeat business and recommendations. Nobody likes to work with a pain in the ass, however talented they are!

4. The Commission: The Low-Down

It is all paying off. Clients are at your beck and call and the phone hasn't stopped ringing since you sent your mailer out! The work is starting to flood in, and then you are asked to quote. Find out how much to charge and how to ask for it, how to manage your time, meet deadlines, and still have a life. What does bleed mean? What are first visuals? What does an art buyer do and why? You are now an image-maker and need to know the full spec on terms and conditions, how long a job should take, what format the artwork should be, and how to get it to your client on time. This section gives you the low-down on how to handle that first commission or how to start handling jobs if you are a hardened pro with bad habits!

1. It makes sense to join an organization that can give you advice when you need it. The Association of Illustrators in London and The Society of Illustrators in New York help members with issues regarding fees, payment problems, and legal matters. Check them out at www.aoi.co.uk and www.societyillustrators.org

2. Quoting fees for jobs is never easy. Try to get a budget from the art director commissioning you. Ask what they have paid for previous work of the same scale, duration, and usage. They normally know what they want to pay.

3. If you need time to think about a fee, say that you will get back to them. Use the time to call fellow image-makers or relevant associations for advice. Put your quote in writing and date it. Get the client to agree to your quote, or amended quote if you agree to adjust it, in writing.

4. Remember, rates depend on a number of issues. It always makes sense to clarify exactly where your work will be used, at what size, for what print run (if applicable), and for what length of time the image is to be used.

5. A general rule of thumb is that advertising work sits at the top of the pile, fee-wise, followed by work for design companies. Book publishers run next, followed by magazines. You could create a small image for an advertising campaign that pays £1,000 ($1,950 US), and the same size image for a mag that brings in £100 ($195 US)!

6. With large jobs it is worth getting a contract sorted before you even start the work. Outline the fee breakdown, with agreed amounts for visuals as well as delivery of final artwork. Put in delivery dates that are realistic. If the client wants it all tomorrow, charge more!

7. Know your rights. If the client rejects your work at visual stage, you can charge 25 percent of the full fee. If they reject on completion, through no fault of yours, go for the full fee. Be prepared to negotiate, though—you may only get 50 percent.

8. Educate your client. The visuals stage is just that. It gives you the chance to show the client what you are planning on doing for the final artwork. It could show the general layout of the image as well as your ideas for how the work communicates. It is not the finished thing.

9. Learn some technical terms. Make sure that you understand the terminology used by your client. If you are not sure what "bleed" is—ask! Don't try and wing it. It will just end in tears.

10. Make sure that you leave the briefing session with all of your questions answered. If not, call the client up when you get back to your studio. It is vital that you understand what you are being asked to do. Leave nothing vague.

11. Check what format they would like to receive the work in—EPS, JPEG—and be sure they can open it. Check what resolution it is expected in, too. Understand why newspapers are different from glossy publications. If in doubt, check it out.

12. Don't trust the colors on your monitor. Check chosen colors against print spec charts. Check how the job is being printed. Will all your chosen colors be easily achieved from the four-color set? Avoid some oranges, as they can go "dirty."

13. If the job requires "specials"—colors printed using specially mixed inks—check that the client has authorized this. Using silvers and metallic colors in your artwork will add to the print cost.

14. RGB or CMYK? Be sure that you format the artwork correctly. Is the image for screen or print? Set your application up properly before you start your job. It is very simple to forget and submit in the wrong format.

15. When you are commissioned to create an image, you sell the rights for its reproduction, unless otherwise agreed. The image-maker retains the ownership of the artwork itself as well as, more importantly with digital work, the copyright. Remember this!

16. You can charge 100 percent of the original fee for the sale of the copyright, but you then lose any rights to the work. Make sure you consider the pros and cons.

5. Studio and Office Tips

It all seems so easy being a professional artist. What could possibly go wrong? Get yourself organized early on to make sure that nothing does. Setting up a studio or office is not just about browsing the Ikea catalog for trestle legs. Keeping the Software Police and the Font Bureau happy, as well as being street legal and paying tax on your earnings, takes organization. Keeping track of your invoices and making sure that your studio is insured, so visitors can't sue when they trip on your portfolio, are basics. Being an artist and a businessperson has to go hand in hand if you are going to avoid pitfalls. Many, often overlooked, issues and tips are covered in this vital section.

1. Get legal; register your business with your local tax office. You are likely to be classified as a Sole Trader and will have to start paying tax on your profits. Get organized right away!

2. Employ an accountant. Best practice is to ask for recommendations. Find one who understands the job of the image-maker. They can then advise on tax-deductible items to keep your tax liabilities down.

3. Invoice for work as soon as it is completed. Make sure that your invoice includes all of the details of the work carried out and to whom you would like the check made out to. And where you would like it sent too, of course.

4. Legally, your invoice must carry an invoice number. You can start the running order at any number. Start at 00100 so that you look as if you've been trading longer!

5. It is likely that your invoice will sit on a couple of desks before it is finally paid. State your payment terms on your invoice and start chasing, on the phone, as soon as that period is up. Start with the accounts department and work your way up the food chain, if you have no luck.

6. Software should be street legal and legit and you should use only fonts that you own. The Software Police are watching you!

7. The life of the image-maker can be lonely. Are you the kind of person who enjoys working on your own in the spare bedroom at home? If not, consider a shared studio. Scan local newspapers for studio space. Shared facilities mean less financial outlay.

8. Get your studio equipped. You will need the following: phone, answerphone, mobile phone, e-mail (with ADSL or ISDN if you are sending artwork down the line), fax (if you produce visuals on paper), CD burner (archive your work as you go), good lighting, and a comfortable chair.

9. Get into a routine. Arrive at your studio, or workspace, at a regular time. Forget the world of daytime TV and get tuned into the reality of checking your e-mail, reading your mail, chasing unpaid invoices, and all other associated tasks before you start actually image-making.

10. Get insured. Get your studio insured. Get your portfolio insured. Insure yourself against injury. Studio insurance covers you if a visitor falls and breaks a leg, and having your portfolio insured means that if it goes missing (quite a frequent occurrence) you get some financial remuneration.

11. Think about the kind of computer you are going to use. A desktop machine tied to your desk in your studio five miles from home may not be ideal if you like to work late into the evening. You may wish to go portable to have the flexibility of working anywhere.

12. Read the design press on a regular basis for news about projects that design companies are involved in and of new companies starting up. You don't have to buy them all; get back to the bookstore or your local library.

13. If you move studio, make sure that people know. A change of address card is a good excuse to send out more promotional material. Obviously, if people don't know how to get hold of you, they won't.

---

6. Perspiration vs Inspiration

You have followed the tips so far. You are a lean, mean, image-making machine. You can hunt down clients, track down new business, quote to within a dollar of the client's true budget. You know shortcuts across town to get you to a briefing in less than five minutes and can call the art director of the latest top style mag by his or her first name, yet still something is missing! Remember that you are an artist. You must feed your habit, too. Stay inspired, stay motivated, and stay busy even when the phone goes dead! Here are some top tips on how to stay an image-maker even when the chips are down.

1. Keep creative. Push your work by adding to your portfolio with work that you want to do rather than just work you are paid to do. You can lead the type of work that you are offered by showing similar examples.

2. Visit exhibitions for inspiration. Look at the work of other image-makers as well as artists and photographers. Examine methods and techniques as well as the ideas in their work. It is a good idea to buy exhibition catalogs, or postcards if your budget is limited.

3. Read more fiction. As an image-maker, you are expected to bring text/copy to life. If you read more and create thumbnail sketches of ideas in response to these texts, you'll keep in practice.

4. Read more factual and nonfiction work. Image-makers need to get under the skin of a subject and understand the issues raised in a writer's text. If you get to grips with the copy, you stand a far greater chance of creating an appropriate image.

5. Go to the theater and the cinema. Engage with dance or opera. Above all else, enjoy other art forms. You can take inspiration from all sorts of sources. It may be as simple as new combinations of color that you see in a theater costume, or the framing of particular images in film. Be inspired!

6. Draw, draw, and then draw some more. Take your sketchbook everywhere and use it in cafes, bars, on the bus, and in the park. If your work does not rely on drawing, but more on photographic imagery, keep your camera with you at all times.

7. Get yourself invited to exhibition private views and meet other artists and image-makers informally. Getting onto a mailing list for a gallery is often as simple as phoning and asking.

8. Check out local groups run by illustrators' organizations. Many groups meet on a regular basis and invite busy professional image-makers to give slide lectures about their work and experiences. Learn from others.

9. If you are really short of work, offer to work as an assistant to a busy image-maker or image-making studio free of charge: you will learn from the experience and pick up more tips. You'll make coffee, mix paints, book couriers, and hunt for reference materials.

10. Use dead time to produce work for competitions. Real dividends can be had from winning or being a finalist in image-making competitions. You can get your work recognized and seen by others, and often an unknown image-maker will come to prominence through this route.

11. Meet other image-makers on a regular basis. Swap stories, contacts, and advice. It is vital that you keep in touch with developments in the image-making world. It is good to have a shoulder to cry on and an audience for your positive stories too.

7. Agents—To Have Or To Have Not

Tired of schlepping around town trying to meet and greet the young guns of the design, publishing, and advertising worlds? Want some other bod to do it for you? For an average of 25–30 percent of each job they get for you, some other bod will. Meet the image-making agent! The dos and don'ts, the good, the bad, and the ugly of the agent are revealed in this section, along with the pros and cons to help assist you in making that choice, and some tips that will help you stand out from the crowd if you decide that an agent is top of your must-have list. What should you expect, what should they expect, and how can you make the relationship as fruitful as possible?

1. Illustration agencies are businesses. To operate, they have to make a profit. This means that they must represent busy image-makers, and plenty of them. If you are not happy being part of this business, go straight to the next section.

2. Still here? Want an agent? Investigate the agencies that are out there. They all have different areas of expertise. Hunt out the one you and your work are most suitable for. Be sure that they operate in the areas of image-making that you do.

3. Be prepared to give up 25–30 percent of your income in commission, but recognize that agents can command higher fees. This may well make up for the commission. If you are lucky enough to be taken on by an agent, check what percentage they take first. Feel free to negotiate.

4. Just like clients, agents are very busy. Don't hassle—be polite. Offer to send samples of your work and wait to hear back when they get the chance to call you. Offer to visit; they will want to meet you if they like your work.

5. Ask the agents you meet about their techniques for getting artists work. Do they rely on just printed publicity? Do they have a Web site? Do they go out and tread the streets with portfolios? Are they proactive?

6. Agents charge (on top of commission) a percentage of the costs of advertising an artist. Make sure you understand how much this may cost you in your first year. Can you afford it? Do they want the cash up front or will they take it from fees owed to you? Check the details.

7. Ask about organized meetings for the image-makers represented by the agency. If they happen regularly, this suggests they have happy artists and is a good sign. It is useful to have a meeting point to discuss issues with other image-makers.

8. Agents may expect to have sole representation of your work. They may want to handle your own clients too. Are you prepared to hand them over? This is another point to discuss before making a final decision.

9. Think carefully about how you present your portfolio at any meeting. Agents will be interested in who you have worked for as well as how your work has developed. They will be thinking about long-term investment. Think the same thoughts!

10. Agents do not tolerate artists working for the agency's clients without declaring it. Some clients are slippery. Don't make the mistake of losing your agent because you have been working behind their back.

8. Getting That Full-Time Job

The life of the freelance, self-employed individual appeared so carefree, didn't it? Start work when you please, take as long for lunch as you wish or even a long weekend— never did like Mondays! That was before the parents/landlord/bank started demanding the rent/mortgage payments and the bicycle/ motorbike/car needed a new tire/windscreen. Suddenly the safety net of a steady wage is far too enticing. You need a job in image-making and fast. Get cracking before the few out there are snapped up! Follow these tips on securing a position and wait for your first monthly pay check to roll in.

1. More and more design companies are starting to employ image-makers or designers who can illustrate on permanent contracts. Check the design press for ads and be prepared to send samples and CV at short notice.

2. Approach publishing companies and greetings card companies if seeking full-time positions. They are still the most likely options. Write a covering letter, introducing yourself and your experience and expertise, and be prepared to follow it up with a phone call.

3. If given an appointment or interview, be on time, be presentable, and know as much as you can about the company. Ask intelligent questions and be keen. These are all fairly obvious tips, but are easily overlooked.

4. Offer to work on a temporary placement basis to gain experience. This is a must if you are a recent college graduate. In return for poor payment, you will get good experience and hopefully a project or two that you can add to your portfolio.

5. Once on a placement, demonstrate yourself to be so good they have to ask you to stay! Don't complain about working long hours—it is the done thing in design and advertising. Get yourself noticed, ask questions, and offer to help others out with presentations.

6. If you want to go into freelance image-making but would like to understand the business in more detail first, try seeking a job at an image-making agency. You'll meet lots of image-makers and clients and see projects through from conception to completion.

7. Another area in which to try your luck is studio management. Be the person responsible for keeping a design studio running. You could be involved in all aspects of the design process. One moment you will be discussing projects with designers, image-makers, and photographers, and the next checking proofs on press at the printers.

8. Keep a record of all contacts while looking for work and after you get the job. These will prove invaluable. All designers and image-makers have favorite printers, repro houses, and places to source reference material, and your list will start to grow. Use your contacts and keep them in an organized fashion.

9. Good Habits

Some tips do not fall into neat little boxes, so here are the best of the rest, the ones that nearly got away. Creating top images, maintaining great promotional material, building a hot portfolio, running a studio and a business takes a lot of skill—make sure that you get into good habits early on. Take time to read this section and follow the instructions carefully. Some may sound obvious, some may appear plain dumb, but, rest assured, they all work. Take daily and complete the whole course. Does exactly what it says on the can!

1. Make sure that your client is pleased with the work that you have produced. Many designers are simply too busy to call to let you know that they have received your artwork. Phone them to check that the work was okay; they'll appreciate it.

2. Don't "lift," "copy," "borrow," or be too "influenced" by the style of another image-maker. Forge your own look. It is the only way to create real, lasting interest in your work. Be original.

3. Make sure that, where possible, you are given a credit for the image-making you have created. If you have a Web address, ask the designer to use it in the credit. It will add to the traffic to your site and lead to more work.

4. Produce work to the deadline given, unless you have an agreed extension. If the deadline appears unworkable, ask for more time before you take on the job. If you spot problems, resolve them early on.

5. Chase up copies of the work when it is in print. Do this as soon as the publication is out. The art director or designer should be happy to send you three or four copies free of charge. These "tear sheets" are what will make up your portfolio.

1

The Lower East Side buzz injects Vault49 with a passion that infects their work and play.

In New York's Lower East Side, on the eighth floor of a building on Ludlow Street, just up from Katz's Deli, the location for the orgasm scene from *When Harry Met Sally*, a large, flatscreen TV awaits unpacking and hooking up to a PlayStation 2. A selection of Macs and PCs buzz semipermanently at Vault49, waking and working hours merging seamlessly as projects stack up from clients across the US and UK. The scene is a million miles away from Vault49's early beginnings or, more accurately, 3,463 miles (5,573km) away.

Jonathan Kenyon and John Glasgow are Vault49. A chance meeting in the screen-print studios of the London College of Printing brought them together. "We met during the final year of our Graphic Design degree, and committed to working together on the rest of our degree projects from February of that year," explains Kenyon. "We developed together; we worked better together than we did when working alone, and learnt the joys of collaborating—something we've never lost."

2

1. Target Practice, promotional project, book jacket design
2. Rogue Shirt, personal project
3. Ludlow Street and Katz's Deli, the Lower East Side, New York City
4. *Good Times 3*, record sleeve
5. Superdoosandsuper, T-shirt design

7   8

10

9

INSPIRE ME

The Vault

Setting up in a Victorian house in South London after graduation, the two continued to create in their preferred medium of screen printing. They named the company after a cupboard under the stairs—the vault—where they kept inks, screens, and squeegees. As for the rest of the name, well, 49 was the house number on the street. "With screen printing being so important to our earlier work and inspiration," Kenyon notes, "it made sense for us to take reference from this in our collective name." The importance of the relationship ensured that names of individuals would not figure in the company title, either. "It was always our intention that Vault49 be a collaborative venture, and we wanted a name that became an entity in itself," he says.

Fueled by their love of print, the two literally took to the streets of London, with self-initiated, screen-printed fly-posters. These led to requests to exhibit at the Dazed and Confused Gallery, run by the style/fashion magazine of the same name, and the coolest watering hole in West London, the Notting Hill Arts Club. The next stage remains a blur; projects flooded in and Vault49 knuckled down to creating a portfolio of work that remains an inspiration. With a client list that included *Time Out* magazine, Levi's, EMI Records, MTV, Honda, Greenpeace, Miss Selfridge, Smirnoff, and Orange, the two decided to make a move.

From the South of the River to the Lower East Side

Relocation to the Lower East Side in the summer of 2004 was not part of any business plan. "It was based on a lifestyle choice," they explain. "It was a personal decision. The bottom line is that we felt young, excited, wide-eyed, and ready for a change, and there was no time like the present." The excitement of being in a new location has not yet waned and inspiration comes from daily life. "Watching the city go past through the windows of an M14 bus, the huge water storage containers on the roofs of Manhattan that look like they're rockets about to launch, the Beastie Boys live at Madison Square Gardens, ice-skating in Central Park, we're no different!" they exclaim.

The Vault49 setting may have changed, and the process of initiating ideas for a new project may have evolved from a "comfy couch with a cup of tea in London" to "hot chocolate on a New-York rooftop with pen and paper," but the essence of how the two work remains the same. A brainstorming session determines whether the pair "take the camera out on the street, make a Google search, or start calling people to collaborate with," explains Kenyon. However, it does all depend on the type of project. "Often we will have a client approach us and be inspired by something that we have already produced, in which case they are already asking us to be guided by a particular visual style in some of our work, although we always push things," he states. "We're pleased to say that we're increasingly requesting and being given the opportunity to set the concept and visual style behind projects, as we seem to be gaining more respect for what we do, and clients place increasing amounts of faith in our ability to design well without being excessively guided," Kenyon adds.

LES Buzz

Just along the street from Vault49 HQ and Katz's Deli is the crossing of Ludlow and Rivington Streets, as featured on the cover of the Beastie Boys' 1989 album *Paul's Boutique*. The Lower East Side remains a magnet. "The buzz is as much to do with the people who congregate here, as the people who live and work here," explains Kenyon. "The LES feels like a social melting pot for creative, energetic people from all parts of New York." Back in the studio, and on the wall is a map of the world covered in pins—places earmarked, perhaps, for another Vault49 relocation in the future.

1
2
3

"Get a studio. Despite the cost, it's well worth it," says Peepshow's Miles Donovan.

"There is a certain rare disease that you contract if you work from home," claims Miles Donovan. "We've all had it in the past and it is not nice; you start cleaning your keyboard with cotton buds during the daytime," he jokes.

Peepshow started life as a Web-based community of fellow image-makers who met while studying together at the University of Brighton in the UK. Initially set up to run simply as "a peep into seven illustrators' folios," the physical studio became a necessity within a few years. "We were all going insane," they admit. "A studio focuses the mind within a work environment. There is more productivity, we can work together on joint projects with ease now, and it's good to actually get dressed and leave the house."

From the original lineup of seven—Miles Donovan, Lucy Vigrass, Andrew Rae, Spencer Wilson, Chrissie Macdonald, Graham Carter, and Chris Joscelyne—the

1. Peepshow at work
2. Peepshow at work
3. Perverted Science, Dreambagsjaguarshoes exhibition, London

4

It was Peepshow's on-screen animation work that caught the eye of KesselsKramer in Amsterdam, while it was hunting for talent for an interesting commission for Italian fashion company Diesel. The Diesel Dream Maker campaign saw 30 global contributors investigate and explore, according to Diesel, "the understanding of human desire and thought" with results that provided a "revolutionary unraveling of the mysteries of the unconscious." Whether the work explored the subconscious as well as the unconscious is unclear, but Peepshow's involvement, an animation entitled "My Disco is Freezing," was considered a dream project, in more ways than one. "No constraints, a budget, well publicized, and we all learnt something new," is Peepshow's take on the experience.

"My Disco is Freezing" follows the strange quest of four figures; a bear, a penguin, and two unidentifiable "munchkins" as they journey across snowy wastelands to a club where the dancefloor doubles as a pool table and origami birds emerge, fluttering, from a woodland scene before an ice-cream van arrives to collect gold bars from a suited man standing by a tree stump. The man is not even given an ice cream for his travels. Surreal stuff, indeed, but a charming, witty, and eminently viewable piece of animation.

group have expanded. Luke Best, Elliott Thoburn, Marie O'Connor, Orko, and Jenny Bowers have all joined the ranks under the common aims of promoting themselves collectively, supporting each other on projects, and working together on group projects and exhibitions.

Naming the group Peepshow was a braver move than first meets the eye; the female group members occasionally receive strange requests from some "clients." "Looking for a different kind of service" is the description put forward by Lucy Vigrass, "if you know what I mean." "Amazingly, we've topped the Google search for 'peepshow' for some time now," adds Donovan.

Prolific Professionals

Peepshow's members are a prolific bunch; each maintains their own individual client lists, working independently on solo illustration commissions for British Airways, Harvey Nichols, Levi's, Evisu, Orange, and Shiseido. As Peepshow, the group client list is not short of top companies, including major advertising agencies such as Ogilvy and Mather, Saatchi and Saatchi, and St. Lukes, as well as the BBC and MTV.

Extra-Curricular Activities

Much of the creative input for Peepshow projects stems from the extracurricular work its members engage in during the group's numerous independent exhibitions. At ultra-cool fashion lifestyle store Dreambagsjaguarshoes they worked on a series of images for "Perverted Science" that hung in frames at various locations throughout the building. At Cake Media they created a permanent installation, working directly on walls and fittings with paints, collage, and stencils, to create a fusion of individual aspects of their varied working ethoi and processes.

5

6

Challenges

Peepshow are not afraid of a challenge. They revel in taking on the unknown and enjoy both their individual commissions and the group projects. An original aim for the group, still valid today, was a simple one: "power in numbers." Watching out for each other, helping and supporting other group members, meant that the act of working together proved successful. "It's an outlet to do whatever you want to do," they insist. "When we started out, we didn't know how far it would go, and whether we would still be doing it five years down the line."

Four years later, Peepshow goes from strength to strength. The studio's busiest day is often Saturday, and with no signs of an early retirement, the keyboard cleaning has been relegated to the evening shift.

7

4. My Disco is Freezing, Diesel Dreams, animation stills
5. Perverted Science, Dreambagsjaguarshoes exhibition, London
6. Perverted Science, Dreambagsjaguarshoes exhibition, London
7. Peepshow HQ, studio entrance

NEW's twenty-fifth floor, tower-block studio looks out upon a sprawling metropolis that awaits carving up via its scooter fleet.

NEW's studio, located high in the air in the heart of south London, allows breathtaking views of the capital that aren't easily matched, but getting to or from the studio is another matter.

Easy Riding

Public transport in London doesn't even come close to its European neighbors; in Paris the Metro runs like clockwork, and in Berlin the subway and tram systems run with military precision. Across the "pond," New York City's subway system, after an investment of millions of dollars, is now showing healthy signs of a full recovery. NEW's solution to the transportation issue in London? Its scooter fleet. This provides the ideal, small, eco-friendly, economical, and hip alternative to a cab, bus, or the subway. "I love the freedom of riding to and from meetings, seeing London live and breath while discovering new streets, shops, people, exhibition spaces …" explains NEW's Austin Cowdell.

1. V Show, exhibition invitation
2. Apathy in the UK, *The Guide* magazine cover, *The Guardian* newspaper
3. NEW, studio interior
4. NEW, *Lowdown Magazine* logo poster

4

7

Visible Processes

It is exactly this freedom of riding the streets that plays into NEW's work—they are very much street-influenced image-makers. "You can have ideas anywhere," continues Cowdell. "Not everyone writes them down or acts upon them, and sometimes developing that idea with a pen, mouse, paint, or 3-D objects is the just the most simple way to proceed." NEW's work has an edge and a gritty visual esthetic that are hard to ignore. "I like to be able to see the processes in the work," comments Cowdell.

Collaboration

The diversity of work that NEW has been involved with continues, adding to an already impressive list. Formed in 1995, the original nucleus of image-makers met while studying together, and quickly formed a group after "scoring some paid design work." The group soon shrank to a tight unit of two, Cowdell teaming up with Matt Hamilton after graduation from college. The NEW studio has undergone a recent mutation, with Hamilton leaving the UK for Australia, and Cowdell now works with a shifting rostrum of illustrators, designers, and image-makers, described simply as a "tag team of collaborators."

These collaborations, in recent years, have included working together on nightclub interiors, magazine designs for John Brown Citrus Publishing, and *Illustrated Ape* magazine, as well as a special project designing rest rooms for a top advertising agency. Another advertising agency allowed NEW and some of its collaborators into their reception areas to run free, creating a unique exhibition entitled The V Show. Across numerous spaces,

the group made images directly onto the surface of the walls, drawing, painting, spraying, and collaging. "When ideas form in your mind, or even if they don't, they're not art, design, illustration, or graffiti. They don't need a classification to exist," insists Cowdell, refusing to allow NEW's creations to be pigeonholed. "It is only when you have to earn money from your ideas that you have to present them neatly labeled. Moving between disciplines is easy otherwise, it is the file-sharing at the end of the process that is the difficult part of being postmodern," he continues with just a hint of irony.

NEW Studios—The Chaos and the Calm

NEW rests on the laurels of its impressive CV. It works constantly, and although it describes the NEW studio as a "relaxed workspace" it is anything but peaceful. The rooftop is littered with radio station aerials, not all legal, the elevators are under constant threat from "local teens honing their graffiti skills," and the NEW scooters are under Cowdell's watchful and protective eyes. "Race-tuned automatic 50cc scooters are very desirable in this part of south London," he explains.

Inside the studio is a different world, with huge modernist windows letting in stacks of daylight and diverse Web-based radio shows filling the speakers until late into the night. "We work on notebooks, scrap paper, beer mats, the backs of bills, letters, important documents, the desktop computer, the laptop—whatever is to hand and feels right," Cowdell states. "Not having a strict formula is best." With that, he dons a full-face motorcycle helmet and takes to the streets for a meeting or a ride with inspiration. He doesn't say which.

Studio Profile: Faile

A design collective, or unit of street artists, with their sights set on sites both at street level and higher.

1

Faile don't advertise their address or their telephone number. Finding Faile's studio isn't easy. Faile communicate via e-mail and the Web, or at least until they are ready to use more traditional forms of contact. Why are Faile so secretive? What are they attempting to protect? The answer lies in their chosen method of visual communication—street art. Not a particularly legal activity in most cities, staying underground ensures anonymity and avoids arrest.

New York, Berlin, London, and Tokyo

Faile's work can be seen on the streets of their hometown, New York City, but their images are equally at home on the streets of Berlin, London, and Tokyo.

1. Exhibition prints, Tokyo
2. Faile publicity shot
3. Will I Ever Find Love? exhibition image, screen print
4. Exhibition image, New York

As well as the street, their large screen prints have graced the walls of galleries and exhibition spaces in many major cities; from street to gallery in a few simple steps. "It's a language. Street art is about connections and relationships," explains Patrick McNeil at Faile HQ. "We've made friendships that have formed because we share an affinity with others using the same media. It's an instinctive thing."

Since forming in 1999, Faile have been active across the globe, but find themselves constantly returning to their base in New York. Canadian-born Patrick McNeil, and Aiko Nakagawa from Japan, run the New York studio, while Faile's third member Patrick Miller, a US citizen, resides in Minneapolis. It is a set-up that works for the group, with McNeil and Nakagawa joining Miller for seasonal printing workshops. "We get together for three weeks at a time to make heaps of new work for shows and for the street," says McNeil. "We all bring different strengths to the group. We form a unit that draws the best of what we bring individually, and it is that energy that creates Faile."

Street Talk

The energy and inspiration that drives Faile's strong graphic language comes from the street, but takes a different tack from most street artists. Bold graphic icons vie for attention, but within the work mixed messages are evident. Where most street art promotes the artist or group behind the work, Faile encourage the viewer to make decisions about what they are viewing. It is, perhaps, Aiko's presence in the group that ensures the visual esthetic takes a more feminine perspective, a rare force in contemporary street art. Mermaids, butterflies, and kids clinging to toy rabbits show the softer side of Faile while barking Alsatians and heraldic crests demonstrate the masculine element of the trio. "We don't want to get stuck on one thing, we are keeping it busy," remarks McNeil. "At the moment we're pretty low-tech and low-budget, but we a have plans."

The Faile Five-Year Plan

Faile's five-year plan embraces a whole host of scenarios. "We want to do films, we want to do movie titles and credits, textile design, graphic design, huge art exhibitions, the lot," enthuses McNeil. Collaborations with like-minded corporate companies has already seen Faile producing clothing ranges for Comme des Garçons and Onitsuka Tiger as well as shoe ranges for Keds and Clarks. "We remix and reuse," admits McNeil. "If a client wants to buy into the art that's fine, but we decide who we work with. Every fashion company wants to collaborate with street artists. They're all trying to apply street credibility to their brands, but fashion pays the bills."

The artistic vision that Faile conjure demonstrates their determination to take on the world. "We want to create a huge art exhibition based around a wrestling event, incorporating the sport into every detail, every aspect of the show, from the masks to the T-shirts, from the ring leader to the posters and tickets," explains McNeil.

Resisting the urge to be categorized, Faile see their mission as bringing together design and art. "The two can exist together," states McNeil. "We don't find that either independent description really encapsulates what we do."

First on the agenda for Faile is a new studio, and not just any space will do. "We need a live/work/office/print-house/home-base/studio," details McNeil. "We need to up the stakes. At the moment the studio we have suits our needs. Our screens are burnt in Brooklyn and we deal in cash; we don't have credit cards." With a new studio, Faile may even start to welcome visitors, or at least give out a postal address.

7

6

8

9

5. Smoke Lady, personal project, limited-edition fashion range
6. Faile, street art, Texas USA
7. Barking Dog, exhibition image, screen print
8. Untitled, *XLR8R* magazine, article
9. Bunny, exhibition image, screen print

1

1. Studio and surroundings
2. Camper Shoes, Joan Brossa in Barcelona
3. *La Vanguardia* newspaper, cultural supplement

Barcelona's industrial quarter, Pueblo Nuevo, is home to laVista —the award-winning studio that is pushing graphic image-making forward in Spain.

"Graphic design in Barcelona," admits laVista's Creative Director, Patrick Thomas, "is still very much in its teens." laVista itself has yet to reach double figures, having been founded only in 1998, by Patrick Thomas and Angela Broggi. Quickly establishing itself as one of Barcelona's most innovative design studios, laVista has been awarded various Gold and Silver trophies in the Spanish National Design awards, and two Silver Art Directors Club, Europe awards for its groundbreaking work.

No Nonsense
Defining approach and working methods is never an easy process, but laVista understand what makes their simple graphic solutions stand out. "We have a no-nonsense approach, we work instinctively, we are antiformula and anti–house style," Thomas explains. "However, there are patterns to our working methods, for example, we are very hands-on at the production stage of any job." This approach pays off—the work coming from the studio is as varied as the eclectic studio itself.

Pueblo Nuevo, from where laVista emerged, has really stepped into the limelight in recent years. As Barcelona's old industrial quarter, the area still has a great sense of the manufacturing base that it once was. laVista works from a vast converted warehouse space on the top floor of a beautiful building that now houses a photographer and a print finisher. Industry still exists in the area, but is now far more connected with communication media.

Keeping the company small and manageable is an aspect of laVista that appeals to both Thomas and Broggi. "There are three of us who work here full-time, with a fourth who looks after laVista Prints," says Thomas. "We try to work 9.00am until 8.00pm. However, it usually turns out to be 8.00am until 9.00pm, with the occasional weekend off."

laVista Prints is a new offshoot which enables Thomas to get back to an original first love—the medium of screen print. Working with other artists, laVista Prints is creating limited-edition signed screen prints with the aim of bringing affordable art to its audience. The first portfolio of work sees Spain's Javier Mariscal, creator of the Barcelona Olympics mascot Cobi, creating work that is both inspiring and quirky. The relationship between Mariscal and Thomas goes back as far as 1991, when Thomas codesigned the Cobi book at Studio Mariscal as a junior designer.

B

2

3

DINERO

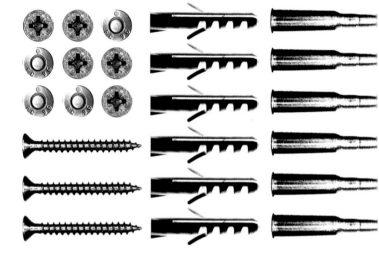

4

5

6

7

Chance Meeting of Minds

It was from a chance meeting with Broggi at a barbecue that the idea to form laVista was born. "We were both working on freelance projects and decided to pool our resources," he continues. "I was impressed with Angela's Apple Mac LCIII with a 25MHz 68030 processor, 4MB of RAM, and 40MB hard drive." It is the strength of the partnership that allows the studio to continue to create strong graphic work, with Thomas taking charge of creative direction and production and Broggi overseeing client liaison and the coordination of projects.

Sleeping on the Job

Working long hours for most days of each week may appear to be a demanding aspect of life at laVista, but Thomas wouldn't have it any other way. "I always have a pencil and notebook, even by the bed. I always try to sleep on a job," he admits. But then bed for Thomas is not far away as he lives in the adjoining studio—work and play are at times almost inseparable. Thomas maintains that there is a divide between the two aspects of his life, however, and two huge sliding doors that reach from floor to ceiling are the proof. As the working day draws to a close, the doors slide open, computers power down, wine bottles are uncorked, and the scent of fresh seafood fills the air as huge paellas are cooked.

The Influence of Catalunya

Barcelona is a city that appears to breathe in laVista's work. The atmosphere and ambience of the capital of Catalunya is often represented in its output. It may be the torn, ripped, and layered posters and fliers adorning the narrow streets off the Ramblas, or the graphic signs on family-run shops that remain decades after their original installation that seep in as inspiration. From wherever it is drawn, the city continues to offer up a never-ending supply of options for a graphic design industry that appears increasingly likely to reach its twenties in fine shape.

1

2

3

Studio Profile: ilovedust

"Do you sell vacuum cleaners?" is a frequent, often crank, but occasionally genuine phone-call request to the studios of ilovedust.

ilovedust's name came about after their first studio's location in a dank, dusty basement environment. "There was dust on everything, all of the time," explains Mark Graham, Creative Director. "We didn't stay long, but the name stuck."

Mark had previously met Ben Beach, fellow Creative Director at ilovedust (ild), at the dust-free environment of Criminal, an independent T-shirt company. The two had decided, while working together on various fashion projects, that their fate would rest with running their own show. Beach's background in designing graphics for T-shirts and Graham's marketing skills (he was originally taken on by Criminal to source new clients), became a crucial combination.

From the original base of two, ilovedust had to expand, as an increasing number of projects began to flow steadily into the studio. Graham and Beach recruited Susie Hetherington and Johnny Winslade as junior designers. Graham is keen to point out the ild working relationship. "There are more of us now," he explains, "but

1. Flowers, promotional project, limited-edition cards
2. Doomed Deer, T-shirt graphic and poster campaign
3. ilovedust studio

4

5

there is no real hierarchy. Our studio setup ensures that we all work together on projects. Design is a personal thing. We tend to all work on all projects, or at least it always starts that way. The way we work means that we all have an input, we put it all in the pot and mix it up."

The design approach for each new project starts with group meetings and discussions and progresses to solo and joint proposals. "From time to time, we arrive at more than one solution we think does the job," Graham concedes, "although if we can't decide which piece works, we let the client decide. "It's as simple as that."

Strong yet Simple

Beach's work as a T-shirt designer has been the backbone of the ild approach: his strong, simple, and graphic work typifies early ild projects. The merge and mix of graphic design and illustration has taken the ild portfolio into uncommon creative outcomes. Clients have recognized the value that ild brings to a project, and its roll call of recent commissions is testimony to this. The group has an impressive client list. An increasingly international blend of avant-garde and mainstream clients

now have faith in the ild philosophy, ensuring that the company continues to work across a broad spectrum. Recent projects have included record industry work for acts such as Charlotte Hatherley and Ash, fashion-related commissions for Diesel and Per Una, and collaborations with graffiti artist Dave White and freshnessmag.com, both based in New York.

The ild studio itself is a creatively cool environment, a far cry from the original basement setup. Now situated a pebble's throw from the beach in the south coast town of Southsea in the UK, it is clear that the location has a positive effect. "Clients love coming to visit us," enthuses Graham. "Many make the trip from London. It's only an hour away but a different world here. We love the place. I grew up here, studied here, and although we may be in meetings in London one day, or over collaborating with artists and designers in New York another, this is where we have our base."

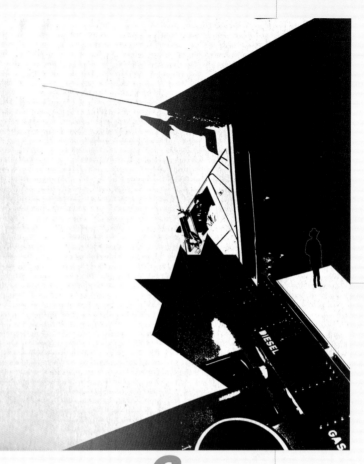

4. 70s Discoteque, *Digital Creative Arts* magazine, cover
5. MX Playtime, *Computer Arts* magazine, feature
6. Midland Convoy, promotional project, limited-edition cards

6

The Dust Doesn't Settle

The studio houses a collection of ephemera gathered because of associations with the designers' interests. These objects help to inform ild projects, too. Limited-edition Japanese Kubrick toy figures nest alongside one-off, handpainted deadstock sneakers in glass-fronted cabinets lining one of the studio walls.

Each ild designer works on a swivel-screen iMac at one long table. This enables each one to receive constant feedback and advice from the others. The studio was designed as a setup that would be conducive to collaboration between its members, and that would enhance the working relationship through the layout of the environment. Early starts and late nights appear to be the order of the day at ild; iTunes mixes kick off at 4.00pm, followed by background reruns on DVD of classic movies such as *Stand By Me, Vanishing Point*, and *Fear and Loathing in Las Vegas*. Creating the right studio atmosphere is second nature. "It's about creating a place that feels just right," admits Graham. With a constant and demanding workload, but incredible energy and spirit, ild are certainly not letting the dust settle.

Contact Details

Ceri Amphlett
ceri@ceriamphlett.co.uk
www.ceriamphlett.co.uk

Jody Barton
work@jodybarton.co.uk
www.jodybarton.co.uk

Tom Barwick
tom.barwick@virgin.net
www.thomasbarwick.com

Luke Best
lukebest22@hotmail.com
www.peepshow.org.uk

Mr. Bingo
mr_bingo86@yahoo.com
www.mr-bingo.co.uk

Stephen Bliss
bliss@rockstargames.com
www.stephenbliss.com

Jenny Bowers
jenny.bowers@virgin.net
www.peepshow.org.uk

Jon Burgerman
jon@jonburgerman.com
www.jonburgerman.com

Paul Burgess
punkrock.paul@virgin.net
www.paulburgessart.co.uk

Anthony Burrill
anthony@friendchip.com
anthonyburrill.com

Brian Cairns
brian@briancairns.com
www.briancairns.com

Graham Carter
mail@graham-carter.co.uk
www.graham-carter.co.uk
www.peepshow.org.uk

Paul Davis
copyrightdavis@hotmail.com
www.copyrightdavis.com

Marion Deuchars
info@mariondeuchars.com
www.mariondeuchars.com

Miles Donovan
m@milesdonovan.co.uk
www.milesdonovan.co.uk
www.peepshow.org.uk

Susannah Edwards
dapper@tesco.net

Faile
info@faile.net
www.faile.net

David Foldvari
info@davidfoldvari.co.uk
www.davidfoldvari.co.uk
www.bigactive.com

Jason Ford
j.ford@macunlimited.net
www.heartagency.com

Lee Ford
Leemforde@aol.com
www.leeford.net

Tom Gauld
tomgaulds.mail@virgin.net
www.cabanonpress.com

Michael Gillette
m.gillette@sbcglobal.net
www.michaelgillette.com

Jasper Goodall
jasper.goodall@sukie.co.uk
www.jaspergoodall.com
www.bigactive.com

Josh Gosfield
josh@joshgosfield.com
www.joshgosfield.com

Phil Hankinson
philhankinson@clara.co.uk
www.heartagency.com

John Hersey
john@hersey.com
www.hersey.com

Nick Higgins
nick.higgins@virgin.net
www.nickhiggins.co.uk

Matthew Green
mail@icantbelieveitsnotbetter.co.uk
www.icantbelieveitsnotbetter.co.uk

Keiji Ito
sato@btf.co.jp
www.butterfly-stroke.com

ilovedust
enquiries@ilovedust.com
www.ilovedust.com

Insect
paul@insect.co.uk
www.insect.co.uk

Rosie Irvine
info@rosieirvine.com
www.rosieirvine.com

Billie Jean
sam@billiejean.co.uk
www.billiejean.co.uk

Kidney
kidnee69@t.vodafone.ne.jp

Tatsuro Kiuchi
me@tatsurokiuchi.com
www.tatsurokiuchi.com

Seijiro Kubo
sato@btf.co.jp
www.butterfly-stroke.com

Joel Lardner
joel.lardner@virgin.net
www.joellardner.com

Chrissie Macdonald
chrissie@chrissiemacdonald.co.uk
www.chrissiemacdonald.co.uk
www.peepshow.org.uk

McFaul
john@mcfaul.biz
www.mcfaul.biz

Joe Magee
art@periphery.co.uk
www.periphery.co.uk

Tim Marrs
tim@timmarrs.co.uk
www.timmarrs.co.uk

Mick Marston
mikiluv@blueyonder.co.uk

Andy Martin
espresso@dircon.co.uk
www.andymartin.uk.com

Richard May
rich@richard-may.com
www.richard-may.com
www.pixelsurgeon.com

Mutador
info@mutador.com
www.mutador.com

Neasden Control Centre
studio@neasdencontrolcentre.com
www.neasdencontrolcentre.com

NEW
thestudio@new-online.co.uk
www.new-online.co.uk

Martin O'Neil
oneill@dircon.co.uk
www.cutitout.co.uk

Peepshow
info@peepshow.org.uk
www.peepshow.org.uk

Simon Pemberton
simon@simonpemberton.com
www.simonpemberton.com

Andy Potts
info@andy-potts.com
www.andy-potts.com
www.blackconvoy.com

Andrew Rae
a@andrewrae.org.uk
www.andrewrae.org.uk
www.peepshow.org.uk

Shonagh Rae
shonagh@shonaghrae.com
www.heartagency.com

Paul Reilly
reilly.p@virgin.net
www.reilly.uk.com

Laurie Rosenwald
laurie@rosenworld.com
www.rosenworld.com

Brett Ryder
brettryder@btconnect.com
www.brettryder.co.uk

Ray Smith
r.smith@c2i.net
www.raysmith.bz

Jim Stoten
jimtheillustrator@hotmail.com
www.jimtheillustrator.co.uk

Studio laVista
patrick@lavistadesign.com
www.lavistadesign.com

Supergympie
supergympie@hotmail.com
www.supergympie.com

Kam Tang
mail@kamtang.co.uk
www.kamtang.com

Elliott Thoburn
ethoburn@btinternet.com
www.peepshow.org.uk

Clarissa Tossin
clarissa@a-linha.org
www.a-linha.org

Aude Van Ryn
audevanryn@onetel.net.uk
www.heartagency.com

Vault49
info@vault49.com
www.vault49.com

Lucy Vigrass
lucy.vigrass@virgin.net
www.lucyvigrass.co.uk
www.peepshow.org.uk

Walnut
mail@walnutatwork.co.uk
www.walnutatwork.co.uk

Paul Wearing
paulwearing@illustrator.demon.co.uk

Spencer Wilson
spencer@spencerwilson.co.uk
www.spencerwilson.co.uk
www.peepshow.org.uk

Steve Wilson
steve@wilson2000.com
www.wilson2000.com

Matt Wingfield
info@mattwingfieldstudio.com
www.mattwingfieldstudio.com

Ian Wright
ian@mrianwright.co.uk
www.mrianwright.co.uk

Index

Acknowledgments

Special Thanks
I would like to thank the following people for their support, patience, and understanding:

Lesley, Louie, Jake, and Felix Zeegen
Russell Hrachovec at compoundEye
Sarah Elliott, Margaret Huber, and all the staff in the
Graphic Design and Illustration Department at the
University of Brighton
Dorothée Fritze
Ondrej Slezek
Lindy Dunlop, Luke Herriott, and April Sankey at RotoVision

Contributors
Many thanks to all the talented people who kindly contributed their work and time:

Ceri Amphlett, Jody Barton,Tom Barwick, Luke Best, Mr. Bingo, Stephen Bliss, Jenny Bowers, Jon Burgerman, Paul Burgess, Anthony Burrill, Brian Cairns, Graham Carter, Paul Davis, Marion Deuchars, Miles Donovan, Susannah Edwards, Faile, David Foldvari, Jason Ford, Lee Ford, Tom Gauld, Michael Gillette, Jasper Goodall, Josh Gosfield, Phil Hankinson, John Hersey, Nick Higgins, Matthew Green (Icantbelieveitsnotbetter), Keiji Ito, ilovedust, Insect, Rosie Irvine, Billie Jean, Kidney, Tatsuro Kiuchi, Seiijiro Kubo, Joel Lardner, Chrissie Macdonald, McFaul, Joe Magee, Tim Marrs, Mick Marston, Andy Martin, Richard May, Mutador, Neasden Control Centre, NEW, Martin O'Neil, Peepshow, Simon Pemberton, Andy Potts, Andrew Rae, Shonagh Rae, Paul Reilly, Laurie Rosenwald, Brett Ryder, Ray Smith, Jim Stoten, Studio laVista, Supergympie, Kam Tang, Elliott Thoburn, Clarissa Tossin, Aude Van Ryn, Vault49, Lucy Vigrass, Walnut, Paul Wearing, Spencer Wilson, Steve Wilson, Matt Wingfield, and Ian Wright.